PLANNING OPTIMAL LIBRARY SPACES

PLANNING OPTIMAL LIBRARY SPACES

Principles, Processes, and Practices

David R. Moore II
Eric C. Shoaf

ROWMAN & LITTLEFIELD
Lanham • Boulder • New York • London

Published by Rowman & Littlefield
A wholly owned subsidiary of The Rowman & Littlefield Publishing Group, Inc.
4501 Forbes Boulevard, Suite 200, Lanham, Maryland 20706
www.rowman.com

Unit A, Whitacre Mews, 26-34 Stannary Street, London SE11 4AB

British Library Cataloguing in Publication Information Available

Library of Congress Cataloging-in-Publication Data Available

ISBN 9781538109403 (hardback : alk. paper) | ISBN 9781538109410 (electronic)

♾™ The paper used in this publication meets the minimum requirements of American National Standard for Information Sciences—Permanence of Paper for Printed Library Materials, ANSI/NISO Z39.48-1992.

Printed in the United States of America

To my mentor,
F. Earle Gaulden, FAIA,
whose love for learning and library design molded me as an architect,
and also to my many library clients who
continually teach, challenge, and inspire me
by their passion for serving others.

—David R. Moore II

CONTENTS

LIST OF FIGURES

FOREWORD

Looking back, previous generations of library planners enjoyed a kind of "good old days." For many years, library space planning was driven by concern for printed materials. Storage came first, followed by other space-intensive print-related needs such as acquisition, cataloging, and easy access for users. As the volume of printed material boomed throughout the twentieth century, library design responded by becoming increasingly industrial in its approach. Efficiency in print management was the standard for success.

Of course, libraries had user spaces that were often beautiful, even inspiring, but judging by their size, placement, and configuration, they were clearly subordinate to concerns for storing all those books. Even the beautiful user spaces were industrial in that attention to efficiency crowded out consideration of what people were actually doing in libraries.

In those "good old days," the relevant variables were few in number, grounded in measurable, physical factors such as volumes held, volumes added, circulation rates, and square-foot allotment for a seated user. All these variables were easy to quantify and predict.

Until suddenly they weren't. The rapid decline of print over the past twenty years took many library planners by surprise. While brick-and-mortar buildings respond slowly to shifting space paradigms, some libraries responded immediately in a purely organic fashion. Sections of stacks were replaced by a few additional tables and chairs, then larger stack areas became potential identifiable user spaces, and then entire floors were being cleared for the same reason. There is nothing organic about this evolution in the present day, where library planning begins with people—and in particular, information users. But now the container of that information is primarily delivered via the Internet to a variety of electronic devices, including computers, tablets, and cell phones. Print management will forever after be a subordinate concern.

When libraries are designed to support information users, planning requires an awareness of a whole new set of variables: pedagogical and learning styles, current and emerging technologies, and cultural expectations. From one point of view, people-focused library planning is messy and continually changing. How wonderful, then, that this transformation in focus simultaneously ended print-based library planning and replaced it with one in which library buildings are better used and more powerfully effective than ever before. The resulting new libraries assert with confidence their timeless role in the presentation, generation, and preservation of knowledge.

Into this crossroads moment comes David Moore and Eric Shoaf's *Planning Optimal Library Spaces: Principles, Processes, and Practices*. Their Road Map approach shows us how to take these messy, amorphous people and information problems and apply a system to engage stakeholders, assess their needs, and produce responsible, flexible, and forward-thinking plans.

Moore and Shoaf take full account of the pragmatic and logistical factors required—budgeting, project phasing options, existing facilities, local context, equipment, and other existing facility considerations. Here, if nowhere else, are constants that no facilities planning process will ever be able to do without.

The Road Map even provides special attention for print storage and management, which will never go away completely. The spectrum of storage options Moore and Shoaf explore are a mirror of the evolving role of those legacy print collections, crucially important in order to map new libraries to the full range of institutional needs. It is worth noting that at one extreme on this spectrum we find robotic, multistory automated storage-and-retrieval systems that must be the ultimate expression of industrial efficiency—and a stark contrast to the human spaces immediately adjacent.

The Road Map approach to library space planning is, like new libraries themselves, firmly rooted in people considerations such as the user behavior factors noted above, but also including internal dynamics such as the political process of identifying campus partners, alliances, and conflicting campus agendas. As an academic library director who has gone through the Road Map

process, I have a special appreciation for Moore and Shoaf's attention to change aversion among some library staff, a complex but manageable aspect of library planning. Here, as in every other way, the Road Map is a manual on how library planning by and for information users can result in transformative design.

Planning Optimal Library Spaces: Principles, Processes, and Practices represents a new approach to library space planning in a rapidly changing technological environment for libraries of all shapes and sizes, both public and academic alike. The book is a top choice for librarians, administrators, trustees, and anyone who has a vested interest in managing and maximizing existing space.

—Stanley Wilder, Dean
LSU Libraries, Louisiana State University

PREFACE

Libraries are constantly redefining themselves. This embrace of change means that libraries and librarians were ready for the sweeping changes of technology that have permeated the profession for the past twenty-five years. The chief problem for librarians is that while they can be flexible with programs, services, and the provision of information, they cannot easily or effectively change the physical environment in which they work. Technological changes have brought a great deal of pressure to rethink library buildings. Librarians in both public and academic libraries have often struggled to convince decision makers to plan and renovate aging library structures to respond to the changes that have come and continue to manifest themselves. A fresh approach is needed—and it has now arrived.

Planning Optimal Library Spaces: Principles, Processes, and Practices describes an innovative approach to planning library spaces and following through with renovations. The new approach to planning and renovating library space described and illustrated in this book has not been presented previously. Each year literally hundreds of libraries engage in major renovations; those libraries are the target audience of this book. They have the need for space and design solutions as well as a plan for estimating costs to present to funders. Furthermore, in many cases libraries can afford an inexpensive Road Map plan but not a wholesale renovation at one time. In those cases, a plan that outlines smaller, sequenced renovations in a phased approach can be funded more easily. Opportunities to renovate in smaller bites as funds become available are very appealing.

The new approach outlined here is geared to both academic *and* public libraries, as the same planning and design principles apply to both, and while we are aware that the number of new-from-the-ground-up libraries is not large, that group is not the target audience of the book. Rather, this book is aimed at those libraries housed in older buildings with solid frames but that have interiors that are out of date; do not meet occupancy codes; lack electrical, networking, and HVAC infrastructure; and are not designed to meet the needs of modern library users. The concepts expressed here will demystify the space planning process, inspire creative thinking, and create hope for the possibility of transforming existing libraries everywhere.

Readers who will glean insight from this text include library directors and administrators, in both the public and academic library sectors, as well as overseers of budgets for those entities. College and university facilities and planning personnel will benefit, as will trustee boards, presidents, and provosts. City and county governmental personnel overseeing public library facilities—such as city managers, mayors, and council members—will benefit from understanding the planning approach as well as ideas about budgeting for renovations as funding becomes available. Architects and space planning organizations will quickly understand and assimilate the planning approach outlined and be able to offer libraries a more flexible and innovative approach to their renovation projects. Furniture manufacturers and designers, retail suppliers, and interior designers will find that their role in providing updated and flexible furniture designs is accelerating and that technology changes require more rapid equipment changes—an important design consideration. Library professional organizations at the regional, state, and national level—especially those that work with smaller libraries or historical societies—will be able to better advocate for construction funding by using the phased approach to renovation that is the heart of the Road Map. Individual librarians reading the book will become equipped to make the case for a library Road Map, better understand trends and influences that make careful planning a necessary and good investment, explain the Road Map process and the principles of a phasing strategy, and understand what goes into a library renovation/construction budget as well as the steps to follow to make the project happen.

The content contained here has been developed over many years, refined, and applied to dozens of public and academic libraries in a variety of contexts. This book begins with a full description of the Road Map approach to library master planning and explains why this is a very different—and superior—approach to traditional library space planning processes. We explore the underlying reasons Road Maps are needed, the common challenges in bringing them to fruition, and the benefits they offer. The Road Map process is broken down into six detailed steps, beginning with the analysis and assessment of the existing library and ending with a budget estimate for the individual phases and the overall Road Map. This book also offers an overview of various print collection storage strategies, noting pros and cons for each, as well as a comprehensive review of the individual elements of a total library budget. Also included is a section on getting started with the Road Map process, which describes how librarians can be part of the initial preparation by evaluating current conditions and identifying low-hanging fruit—steps that can be taken easily for immediate progress. Finally, we present Road Map case studies that include actual before-and-after floor plan drawings and carefully described phasing plans for a variety of academic and public libraries of different sizes and configurations. Throughout the text, comments from library directors highlight their own success stories using the Road Map approach.

Planning Optimal Library Spaces: Principles, Processes, and Practices offers an innovative approach to renovating libraries that results in increasing the functionality, efficiency, and capacity of existing facilities. As library planning for renovation moves forward, it is especially important to create spaces that not only provide for the changes in use libraries have experienced, but also ensure flexibility and adaptability for future changes. The Road Map planning approach allows existing libraries to achieve their highest and best use with limited funds. It is a manual that librarians, administrators, and decision makers can share to communicate with and inspire action in those who fear that doing anything is unaffordable.

ACKNOWLEDGMENTS

I want to thank my clients for entrusting me and my team with your libraries—it is a privilege and an honor. To those of you who, along the journey, evolved from clients into my friends and trusted advisers, it is our relationships that I value the most. You know who you are!

I am indebted to and want to thank my fellow principals at McMillan Pazdan Smith Architecture, especially our executive team: Ron Smith, Brad Smith, Joe Pazdan, K. J. Jacobs, Karen Calhoun, and Chad Cousins. Your support for this book is humbling, and your wisdom, hard work, and high values have built an incredibly creative, dynamic, and rewarding place to practice architecture and a place where ideas take shape every day. I am truly blessed and privileged to be surrounded by—and to work alongside—the most talented and professional team of architects and designers I have ever had the pleasure of working with. Your creativity, passion, and commitment to serve our clients makes our work even more meaningful.

Thank you Amanda Gascon, Rick Connor, Ben Wofford, Edgar Mozo, Haley Balentine, Melissa Carroll, Travis McConkey, Caitlin Sexton, and Jessi Kendall Marks—without your contribution of countless hours and creative energy, this work would not be a reality.

Finally, I would like to thank God for his blessings, mercies, and grace, and the gift of my family. Thank you for your love and constant encouragement. I love you dearly.

—David

I would like to thank everyone from Everett Library at Queens University of Charlotte, David Moore of McMillan Pazdan Smith, Marc Bove of the Bommarito Group, Bill Nichols, Troy Luttman, and Claudia Cardenas.

—Eric

1

INTRODUCTION TO MASTER PLANNING AND THE ROAD MAP APPROACH

The vast majority of Americans believe public libraries serve their communities' educational needs pretty well. In fact, it has been written that "it seems that nearly everyone who's been to a local library at least once in their lives approves of them" (Robinson 2016). Public libraries have always been and continue to be the most accessible path to the world's information, and today they are important providers of learning-related programs that are specifically designed to supplement their communities' local educational ecosystems. Whether offering early literacy programs or providing job resources and access to high school certification programs, public libraries are at the heart of their communities, and the depth of services offered is unprecedented. Libraries must adapt and evolve to keep up with their community's changing needs and the world around them.

Likewise, academic libraries serve as their institutions' intellectual heart, providing a stimulating place where students, faculty, and staff can engage in collaboration, discovery, research, and sharing while simultaneously finding areas for quiet, contemplative solitude. These libraries are expected to be premier facilities featuring well-designed spaces that attract and retain students and faculty. They are the "third place" for their communities of users, offering a space to hang out, socialize, and reflect in repose. They should promote lifelong learning, feature innovative teaching spaces, and be equipped with the latest audiovisual resources and technologies.

Despite their popularity and the vital role they play in their communities, most libraries were designed and built in a different time for different purposes. Many are now out of date, lacking modern facilities and in need of renovation, redesign, and reinvention. These libraries can decide to make the most of their current facilities rather than accept the status quo. They can choose to just make do, or they can move forward by taking a closer look to ensure their facilities are being used as efficiently and effectively as possible. The best way to do this is to develop a plan that looks at the big picture.

Plans that look at the big picture are known as *master plans*. Communicating a future vision, library master plans can be inspirational documents that offer hope and unify efforts. Unfortunately, however, many come with such high price tags, lengthy implementation periods, and lack of flexibility that they are soon shelved or become antiquated before their full vision is realized. This often results in squandered energy, hope, and excitement. Seen as all-or-nothing propositions, traditional library master plans can seem too pie-in-the-sky to invest time and money to develop.

As economic pressures on library funding sources result in cutbacks, delays, and deferred projects, libraries struggle to maintain important services, operating hours, and staff. When this happens, the natural instinct is to hunker down and retreat into survival mode. Aspirations for new, renovated, and expanded facilities are put on the back burner even though demands for increased space and services continue. Through the Road Map approach to library master planning, however, planners may find that achieving the best and highest use of these facilities is as simple as rearranging furniture, spring cleaning, or collection analysis. In almost every case, this requires thinking outside the box and being free from "this is the way we've always done it" syndrome.

The Road Map approach to library master planning articulates a future vision with an incremental, phased strategy and offers options for more immediate ways to improve functionality, efficiency, and capacity. The print repositories of the pre-technology past need to be transformed sooner rather than later, and the Road Map is a useful tool to help make that happen.

The purpose of this book is to demystify the Road Map approach to library master planning, inspire creative thinking, and create hope for transforming existing libraries everywhere.

2

WHY THE ROAD MAP APPROACH?

A CASE FOR MASTER PLANNING LIBRARIES

If you don't know where you're going any road will get you there.

—Lewis Carroll

A

B

Figure 2.1. (a) L'Enfant's master plan for Washington, DC, 1792; and (b) Oglethorpe's master plan for Savannah, Georgia, 1818. Both plans established a framework that is still evident today.

Pierre Charles L'Enfant's plan for the city of Washington, DC, later developed by Senator James McMillan, has informed and shaped the growth of the nation's capital for more than two hundred years. This created a framework for grand public spaces and monumental architecture, including the National Mall as we know it today. Likewise, James Oglethorpe's plan for the city of Savannah, Georgia, utilized wards, blocks, and public squares organized through an orthogonal grid to plan for the city's growth for nearly two hundred years. In

both cases, master plans established centuries earlier are still apparent and relevant. They provided a rational organizing framework, yet offered enough flexibility to accommodate inevitable growth and change over time.

Today, most of us encounter master plans in the context of new commercial developments, governmental public spaces, or academic campuses. There is an entire industry dedicated to the master planning of college and university campuses, whose plans must be updated, revised, and rewritten on a regular basis. Likewise, city and county master plans are written and revised regularly and updated to reflect new development and growth patterns. In every case, master plans provide a framework for future improvements and articulate a vision for space development by serving as a guiding document to be referenced and followed.

Master planning individual buildings is perhaps less common, but with regard to libraries is absolutely necessary and immensely invaluable. Libraries are not as large as cities or college campuses, but in many ways are equally complex. Libraries must adjust and adapt to constant changes that include new community service programs, evolving pedagogies, new media and technologies, and so on. In order for libraries to successfully adapt and remain relevant, they must have a plan.

The Road Map approach to library master planning offers a new method to prepare for the future. One librarian described the Road Map this way: "It is a vision, a narrative, a story about a preferred future in action." This captures the notion that a Road Map is intended to be active, not static. It evolves as the story and narrative of the library changes. Another librarian described it this way: "I think of the Road Map much like a playbook; I refer to it often and in response to issues and needs that arise throughout the year." The Road Map is a tool that enables libraries to move beyond their present situation.

It is not uncommon to become inoculated to the surrounding environment. It becomes difficult to see opportunities (or shortcomings) that are obvious to a fresh set of eyes in much the same way as a proofreader finds glaring mistakes in a paper the author has read a hundred times. Sometimes people become so invested in planning decisions made in the past that they are unable to see the need to change and adapt, and the thought of wholesale change at times can seem daunting. Whatever the case, maximizing a library's functionality, efficiency, and capacity through an effective,

well-thought-out Road Map is a welcome notion, but for many, whether it is possible or how to go about it is a mystery.

CONSTANT CHANGE

It's not the strongest species that survive or the most intelligent, but the ones most responsive to change.

—Charles Darwin

"The only thing that is constant is change" is a quote we are all familiar with. Libraries have endured immense amounts of change in a very short time. The library has always been—and continues to be—the place where one could go to find and access information; today, however, it is also the place where one can go to create and share that information. Today, information is found in a variety of media not necessarily tied to the library's physical location, whereas in the past, information found in a library was intrinsically tied to its materials and collections.

Because of this, libraries used to amass large collections "just in case" an item might be needed. Today, libraries focus on strategies to provide information "just in time" by creating pathways to finding information precisely when it is needed. Simply said, libraries have evolved to become places for people, not property. Rather than warehouses for books, libraries are now portals to the world of information available through digital time and space. Although there are still books and audiovisual materials on the shelves, vast resources are available "in the cloud" that may be accessed from anywhere in the world. Unlike the static design of libraries in the past, modern libraries must be designed to accommodate constant change as they evolve to remain relevant to the communities and campuses they serve.

Figure 2.2. Evolution of technology

DRIVERS OF CHANGE

Today, public and academic libraries alike must adapt to ever-evolving technologies, respond appropriately to changes in user habits, reevaluate services provided, and address modern security concerns that focus more on the protection of those within the library than of its materials. How a library responds to these drivers of change forms the basis for the development of a comprehensive Road Map that will inform and illuminate a path forward.

Technology

Libraries are often under scrutiny by governing and administrative authorities who question why libraries are needed now that "we can find everything on the Internet." As technology changes the way space is used and information is organized, stored, and accessed, library leaders must carefully envision and clearly articulate the ongoing role of the library within its campus or community to justify it.

There is no doubt that technology is a driving force behind change in libraries. Enabling technology requires changes to a building's infrastructure as well as to how people access and obtain the information they seek. Technology impacts the furniture and organization of materials inside the library—and the space needed to contain it. The rapid rate of change exacerbates the situation, making it more difficult for libraries to keep up: What is current or cutting edge when a building is designed can be outdated by the time it opens. Because of this, many libraries find themselves constantly behind the curve.

> As a new library director at my institution, one of my earliest conversations with my provost was about a long-range plan for the library. It was clear to us that in order to meet the needs of today's library users, the concept of a library as a book repository was not going to work either in our present or future. We needed a plan that would accommodate more collaborative learning and technology use, while also being a place for quiet, contemplative study as well as a place to hold collections. (Leah Dunn, University Librarian, UNC Asheville)

Habits

The needs and habits of library users are changing. The questions asked, the spaces sought, and the services required are very different than they were even a decade ago, and librarians are scrambling to respond. On academic campuses, pedagogy is also changing, with a focus on collaborative learning, integrated research, and the creation of artifacts that demonstrate knowledge. Public libraries, along with coffee shops and commercial book stores, serve as remote offices for many in today's highly flexible job market. Those seeking employment and pursuing entrepreneurial endeavors often utilize the library's job centers and coworking spaces as well. For many, the library remains the preferred destination for solitude and escape from the distractions of technology, while at the same time the same individuals—ironically—scour the building in search of power receptacles to recharge their electronic devices.

> The biggest driver for redefining our library through the Road Map process is probably pedagogy. Because teaching is happening differently, it is affecting user needs and demands, and the tools that they use to be successful in their coursework. Assignments that students come to the library to complete now are much more varied than they were before. Students come in with a ten-page research paper, but are now required produce a two-minute video clip instead of, or in addition to, their paper. They might need a 3-D model of what they are studying, or they are building the technology needed to solve a research problem. More often than not, they are working on these assignments in teams. (Leah Dunn, University Librarian, UNC Asheville)

Services

The services librarians must provide, and which the building must support, are rapidly changing in an attempt to keep up with technology and new demands from users for services, equipment, and space. The library staff is under constant pressure to stay current with Internet-driven resources, and challenged to cross-train, retool, and learn additional skills. Traditional reference questions are fewer, and more information is delivered through online databases, accessed through streaming, and downloaded onto mobile devices. Librarians must manage collaborative smart classrooms, small-group study rooms, makerspaces, recording studios, media labs, and even cafés. As libraries incorporate new and additional services, the buildings must adapt; often, however, librarians just make do with what is available.

> Our building design was based on a late 1980s definition of a library. This means that it was primarily a repository for books, with also an eye towards individual, quiet study. We had lots of stacks. Most of our areas were big, open areas where any sound that is produced is

amplified across the whole floor. It had multiple service desks for functions that were no longer provided in the way in which they were designed for originally. Electrical outlets were few and far between. We needed a space where groups of people could collaborate without being disruptive to others. And we needed spaces where people could utilize technology effectively. Space for quiet, contemplative study still has its place, but it has to coexist with spaces that are used for these other purposes as well. (Leah Dunn, University Librarian, UNC Asheville)

Many university libraries are finding that students and faculty benefit greatly by unifying their services in one location rather than staffing several service desks throughout the library. At San José State University, we consolidated five service points on different floors into one location on our first floor. Now users can now go to one location to ask for assistance on any topic, including how to print, locate microfilm, check out a book, or utilize special collections. Our goal is to provide seamless, user-friendly service. This does not mean that the first person they talk to is the person who answers their question. Instead, they are connected with the expert who can help them. Rather than having to find the expert, the expert is brought to them.

The unified service point model provides great efficiency in staffing. Instead of library employees sitting passively at a desk, they can be actively reaching out to library users across campus, or developing much needed digital tools and resources. The unified service model also increases the expertise of library employees and provides an opportunity for organizational learning. By engaging experts in technology, research, access services, special collections, and other services in one area, library employees are exposed to a wealth of information. Continuous assessment of service delivery within this model is essential. (Tracy Elliott, PhD, MLIS, University Library Dean, San José State University)

Security

In the past, library security was focused on eliminating the theft of library property, and a number of approaches were used over the years to protect books, printed materials, audiovisual resources, and other collection-based library property. Now, however, security measures have shifted to focus more on the people inside library facilities, both users and staff alike. Public awareness of security concerns in everyday life has grown concurrent with social media and personal communication devices; there is also a sense among library users and staff that gun violence is on the rise. Concerns for the safety of individuals in both public and academic libraries is a real concern.

Most older library buildings do little to address these safety concerns. Many libraries have remote areas that are not directly visible from service desks or security personnel, and very few have automatic locks for doors, electronic swipe cards that track time and date of access, or silent alarms to summon security assistance. Often, ranges of library shelving hinder visual access through the building rather than enhance it. The library has always been a place where visitors expect to feel and be safe. For libraries to meet the needs of their communities, they must address these concerns and improve security deficiencies using the Road Map process (see figure 2.3).

LIBRARY SAFETY AND SECURITY

A variety of issues are causing public facilities and university campuses to rethink their approach to safety and security, and libraries are a part of this as well. Unfortunately, shootings and other acts of violence have permeated society and have occurred in and around libraries. In response, public safety professionals encourage space planners to conduct a "Crime Prevention through Environmental Design" (CPTED) study.

CPTED is a multidisciplinary approach where proper design of a building helps with the reduction of incidents and makes users feel more comfortable in their surrounding environment by creating a welcoming and warm atmosphere. CPTED attempts to reduce those undesirable behaviors by using environmental elements such as controlling access, promoting opportunities to see and be seen, and defining ownership. CPTED is truly a collaborative, approved effort involving campus public safety, architects, building occupants, and end users. In planning for the security of the library there are several things to consider:

- **Addressing large and small rooms.** Smaller rooms leave less space in which to shelter in place.

- **Identifying high-volume versus low-volume room security concerns.** Rooms that receive a lot of use–the instruction lab or copy center, for example–may be more clear-cut targets.

- **Balancing personal safety and group safety.** Individual lockable study carrels might keep more people safe, but are not always practical or warranted in libraries. Especially as space design moves toward greater flexibility and openness, one expects to find larger groups of library users.

- **Roaming patrols between library staff and public safety personnel.** Often one of the best prevention methods is a highly visible security presence.

- **Placing security cameras in strategic locations.** Proper design means that any and all exits from the building have cameras that can provide detailed images. As most know, security cameras are not necessarily for prevention but do offer video documentation before, during, and after an incident.

- **Evaluating current or new access control options for optimal benefit.** The use of card swipe security for doors has increased in many locations. For spaces that have not yet added them, a renovation is the right time to look at issues related to cost, operation, cabling, and connecting a card swipe system to any existing data management and information technology infrastructure.

- **Layering security options to make it more difficult for potential violators.** This means creating impediments that make it difficult and time-consuming for an attacker to easily move through a space. This discourages a potential attacker from targeting the library.

- **Designing the right fire detection and suppression systems (e.g., sensors for water leaks).** Newer systems are available that are more accurate than before. Depending on the size and scope of the renovation, a sprinkler installation may be required by local fire safety codes.

- **Training for library staff related to emergency situations such as inclement weather, fires, active shooters, and general evacuation procedures.** This is not a complete list of factors to consider (space planners can help with decisions about unique aspects of individual library buildings), but it does provide an example of how safety and security in the library can be improved dramatically using the CPTED study approach.

–Ray Thower
Assistant Vice President, Public Safety & Campus Police
Queens University of Charlotte

Figure 2.3. Library safety and security

CHANGE MANIFESTATIONS

Digital Impact on Print Collections

Figure 2.4. As print materials become accessible digitally, it is not uncommon to see empty shelving. Five empty DF shelving units are equivalent to one small group study room.

Libraries have been moving their acquisition budgets away from print and toward digital electronic resources since the early 1990s. Although this transformation started slowly, the result is that much less space is required for print materials within the library. When print materials are removed, empty shelves and gaps in the collection remain, resulting in underutilized shelving (see figure 2.4). If captured, the space occupied by this shelving could be repurposed for new types of user spaces.

Material Focused to People Focused

Figure 2.5. Libraries are creating spaces primarily focused on user comfort, not just spaces to store materials.

Traditional libraries were built to house print-based materials in the form of books and periodicals, as well as audiovisual media. The space required for these materials comprised at least half the total space available within a library, and sometimes much more. The availability of content through the Internet and the rise of smartphones and other personal electronic devices have changed this. Materials are no longer the top consumer of space in the library. As the availability of content and information through streaming and digital downloads increases, sole reliance on physical materials is lessened. Because of this, physical space within the library can be leveraged to create new spaces that enable new activities such as creation and makerspaces, innovative teaching and learning environments, and creative programming and support service zones, as well as areas for rest and relaxation (see figure 2.5).

Seating Variety

Figure 2.6. Examples of different types of seating found in the James B. Hunt Jr. Library at North Carolina State University

Gone are the days when libraries were limited to three general types of seating: reading tables and chairs, lounge seats, and study carrels. In public and academic libraries alike, as users spend more time performing a diverse array of activities, it is important that the furniture in each space be comfortable and conducive to the specific task at hand. Furniture in today's libraries is flexible and reconfigurable to accommodate tasks that span from a few minutes to hours on end. See figure 2.6 for an example of the variety of furniture in one library.

Collaboration and Group Study

Figure 2.7. Collaborative learning environments with flexible furniture, movable marker boards, and a variety of group configurations

Learning has changed over the years, and collaborative learning is now well-integrated in the primary grades. When students reach adulthood and either attend college or enter the workforce, they are now accustomed to learning while sharing with each other. Figure 2.7 is an example of popular student study environments. Collaborative exchange is part of several new learning approaches that incorporate technology and the Internet into classroom environments. Libraries, which function as learning environments, are seeing growing demand for collaborative space. This represents a move away from older models, where libraries dedicated much of their space to quiet and solitary contemplation. Creation of new collaborative spaces and associated adjacencies requires careful planning.

Quiet Space and Individual Study

Figure 2.8. (a) Posts on a student input board in an academic library expressing the desire for quiet spaces; (b) individual study nooks in the quiet room at Grand Valley State's Mary Idema Pew Library

Libraries have always been synonymous with "quiet," and everyone is familiar with the stereotypical "shushing" librarian with a raised index finger in front of pursed lips. While definitions about what constitutes quiet may vary from generation to generation, there is no question that the demand for quiet spaces within the library is on the rise. Figure 2.8 is an example of individual quiet study nooks within a larger quiet room where silence is strictly enforced by the room's occupants.

Users seek places within the library that are free from the buzz of conversational collaboration, socializing and cell phones, printers and copiers, makerspace noise, and all the other sounds that many consider to be the soundtrack of daily life. Libraries are creating intentionally quiet and comfortable spaces that are reserved for solitary thinking and study—and that can coexist with the noisier activities contained within.

Self-Service and Changes in Service Delivery

Figure 2.9. Examples of consolidated service and self-service options at an academic and public library

As libraries focus more on the user experience, they seek creative ways to make their users feel welcome and able to more easily get the help they need. Libraries are gravitating to a single or unified service point rather than the multiple help desk approach whenever possible to offer better, more personal service. By trading names like *Circulation*, *Reference*, or *Periodicals Desk* for more user-friendly terms such as *Help*, *Info*, or *Concierge Desk*, libraries attempt to be more approachable, intuitive, and less intimidating (see figure 2.9).

By consolidating their points of service into single, centralized locations, libraries are able to receive and assist library users more directly, rather than shuttling them to a variety of specialized desks scattered throughout the library. Not only do fewer specialized desks free up staff for more important purposes, it also builds on user interest in self-service, with the understanding that help is available if needed. Many libraries now utilize self-service scanners, checkout devices for circulating materials, and automated material handling systems, as well as online room reservation systems and other self-serve applications.

Library as Third Place

Figure 2.10. Local coffeehouses are good examples of third places in a community.

Ray Oldenburg, in his book *The Great Good Place*, describes the *third place* as the next most important social surrounding in a community after a person's home (the first) and workplace (the second; Oldenburg 1999). Third places are often described as neutral places that are free, accessible, visited by regulars, welcoming and comfortable, and have available food and drink (see figure 2.10).

Third places are open and accessible to all, and in many ways are a person's home away from home. They are places where people do not *have* to be, but where they *want* to be when they are not at home or at work. Libraries are competing with commercial enterprises to be their users' third place, and so they should be designed to offer a human connection and convey a sense of warmth, belonging, and community.

Creation Studios and Makerspaces: "Hands-on Learning"

Figure 2.11. Different types of tools and equipment found in makerspaces in both public and academic libraries

The library used to be a place where one went to get information, but today one can also create content and share it at the library. Libraries have embraced learning through activities for decades, as evidenced by the evolution of the public library children's program room. What began as a space for story hour evolved into a place where literacy and other skills were taught and learned through acts of creation. Libraries have now embraced the idea of having spaces that allow users of any age to participate in acts of creating as a means to educate, learn, and explore. Figure 2.11 illustrates makerspaces in both public and academic libraries.

In public libraries, these spaces can facilitate activities from quilting to garden club demonstrations to culinary kitchens to workshops, and many even incorporate digital equipment such as CNC (computer numerical control) machines, 3-D printers, and vinyl cutters. Libraries are recognizing that studio environments in which individuals can work, independently or in groups, to share, critique, and collaborate throughout the process lead to richer and more effective learning and retention of information (see figure 2.12).

THE MAKERSPACE IS MORE THAN A "MAKER SPACE"

Some trace the makerspace idea in libraries to 2006, noting that it grew out of a rising do-it-yourself culture enabled by information freely and widely disseminated on the Internet. While development of makerspaces in libraries continued with advances in computer-aided design (CAD) that allowed for design and production of 3-D products produced using specialized equipment, a makerspace is much more than a room with 3-D printers. These may be more accurately referred to as creative spaces, and their history in the library probably has roots in classrooms that developed for learning a variety of skills, facts, figures, and topics. Meeting rooms at public libraries were used to teach knitting in the 1920s. They were used to teach the Dewey Decimal System in the 1950s. Typing rooms were found in most academic libraries as late as the 1970s. And if these are not the same as today's makerspaces, it is less about the use of the space than it is the focus on the user of the space.

Until recently, the focus of the makerspace has been on the equipment available, whether a 3-D printer, a sewing machine, or a video production studio. Attention must be given to the design of the space so that it supports and promotes interactivity between the user and his or her team, the equipment, the design software, and the library support personnel. The purpose of these spaces is the construction of artifacts and the enabling of rapid prototyping to advance an idea or concept. They promote learning by doing and are collaborative in nature and design. Users in these spaces will need help and assistance from library staff to understand software and to learn techniques for production and for using equipment. These needs will change over time and will drive changes to the space itself. Put succinctly, the maker makes the makerspace.

Images A, B, and C depict makerspaces and available tools and materials in Stanford University's d.school.

Already a decade into the makerspace phenomenon in libraries, several aspects related to planning this type of space have emerged:

- Available lighting and availability of power, including drop chords from ceiling

- Sufficient space to accommodate a variety of activities

- Durable, easy to clean finishes

- Mobile organizing furniture to make clean up easy and to promote safety

–Eric Shoaf, MLS, MPA

Dean of the Library
Queens University of Charlotte

Image A

Image B

Image C

Figure 2.12. The makerspace is more than a "maker space."

Digital Media Studios

Figure 2.13. Spaces to capture and create digital content

With evolving technologies, users are adapting to a host of creative tools from Adobe, Apple, Google, and others to develop presentations, videos, and other multimedia artifacts that demonstrate learning and highlight practical skills to potential employers. Additionally, students and users require peripheral hardware such as cameras, green screens, microphones, lighting, musical equipment, mixers, and recording devices to capture and create media-rich digital content.

In response, libraries are adding spaces that accommodate the use of digital media hardware and software. Digital media studios can combine the help and technology typically associated with an information commons and a creative environment typically associated with makerspaces to create specialized spaces with proper acoustics and lighting. Examples of these types of spaces are included in figure 2.13.

These spaces require librarians and staff to be fluent in the operation of equipment, savvy in understanding software, and, in many instances, cognizant of the need to create online repositories to provide a permanent home for the digital artifacts created therein. In the past, the concern was having enough square footage to shelve all the print material; now there is equal concern about having adequate server space for video and other digital artifacts.

Information/Learning/Research Commons

Figure 2.14. Examples of partner and student help spaces commonly found in public and academic library commons spaces

Information commons spaces that blend library research and IT help have become common in many academic libraries, and most are gravitating—if they haven't already—to the learning commons model, which includes academic support partners such as writing centers, tutoring, academic success centers, student support services, and supplemental instruction (see figure 2.14). Research libraries are also creating research commons that are geared more specifically to graduate students and faculty. One librarian described a research commons this way:

> The "research commons" area of a university library is a physical representation of not only how the library supports the research and scholarship on campus, but of the actual research and scholarship output. Also sometimes referred to as a scholar's commons, they break down the research silos that happen in academic departments across campus and are academically neutral. Scholars across campus can work side by side with colleagues from other disciplines represented at a university. For instance, the anthropologist might be getting assistance with data analysis software in the same space that an engineer is utilizing data visualization software. All researchers on campus can display and share their work in the same place, allowing for potential collaboration across disciplines. Libraries are essential for providing access to knowledge [and] therefore are the natural place for sharing the knowledge created by the university faculty, researchers, and students.
>
> Spaces found in a research commons may be designed to accommodate any or all of the following: data visualization, research symposiums, research consultations, negotiating author rights, discovering research funding, developing data management plans, using data software tools, displays of research outputs, publishing, measuring research and scholarship impact, and any other resources and services which support the research lifecycle. (Tracy Elliott, PhD, MLIS, University Library Dean, San José State University)

The notion of partners with synergistic missions coexisting in the library is also gaining popularity. IT services (either in whole or as part of a help desk operation), faculty success centers where new approaches to pedagogy are taught and integrated into course management systems, and student disability services that provide everything from Americans with Disabilities Act (ADA) assistance to test-taking stations to study locations are examples of such partnerships.

In public libraries, commons-type areas manifest themselves more as open social space with collaborative community environments and digital access. Partnership with community organizations that align with the library's mission and can assist with programming often leads to innovative spaces for user assistance such as literacy, continuing education, job centers, career counseling, coworking and entrepreneurial incubator spaces, and so on (see figure 2.15).

LIBRARIES AND COMMONS: LABELS AND DEFINITIONS

In 1997, when I was hired as head of the first information commons (IC) in the UNC system, I found only a few ICs across the United States to learn from. All had arisen from the ashes of failed attempts to situate generic computer labs in traditional reference departments. Librarians had been ill-prepared to cope with student demands for seamless transitions from database research to project completion. Students had begun exiting libraries to work in computer labs. By devising this new service model to give students "one-stop shopping," ICs had shown dramatic results in reversing that exodus, and their door counts soared. By 2000, these early successes had drawn notice across many campuses. A convergence of other learning support activities–tutorial services, writing centers, and media labs–began considering ICs as potential "hub" locations where their staff might serve students "at point of need." The commons began to morph from a library-centric place to a shared space where librarians, tutors, faculty advisers, and media experts could collaborate. Simultaneously, the label *information commons* began to give way to the new label *learning commons* (LC).

In my 2004 white paper for the IC conference at Southern Cal, I suggested that an IC may be defined as "being library-centric, featuring a cluster of network access points and associated IT tools situated in the context of physical, digital, human, and social resources organized in support of learning." I then suggested that an IC becomes a Learning Commons "when its resources are organized in collaboration with learning initiatives sponsored by other academic units, or aligned with learning outcomes defined through a cooperative process." These definitions were soon adopted by other researchers, such as Russ Bailey and Scott Bennett. It is not hard to find spaces still labeled IC that better fit the LC definition. Does that render the labels meaningless? No, because long-range assessment studies support the notion that some library commons remain more library-centric, while others move toward more collaborative arrangements. This depends more on institutional culture than it does on whichever label was applied at the outset. So the definitions and the labels have proven useful as assessment tools, regardless of what label an individual library may prefer.

Since 2005, new and more sophisticated digital tools and services have emerged to support faculty and graduate-level research in such endeavors as the digital humanities, data curation, knowledge visualization, and interactive multimedia. In moving to incorporate these more advanced tools for use by faculty and graduate students, a number of university libraries have adopted labels like research commons (RC). Ohio State University's RC Task Force issued a report (8/15/13) that points the way toward a definition of this newest commons model:

Research commons are spaces, either physical or virtual, that provide connections to services and resources that support faculty needing consultations about digital publishing or managing data resulting from their research, graduate students needing assistance with specialized data needs. By providing a suite of consulting services, in a single location, with appropriate expertise and collaborative, technology-enhanced spaces, the research commons offers the possibility for sharing ideas around emerging research.

–Donald Beagle

Director of Library Services
Belmont Abbey College

Figure 2.15. Libraries and commons: labels and definitions

Specialized Teaching Spaces

Figure 2.16. (a) Edgar Brown Digital Resources Laboratory at Clemson University, a campuswide high-tech classroom; and (b) iPearl Immersion Theater, (c & d) Creativity Studios, and (e) Teaching and Visualization Lab at North Carolina State University

Academic libraries are becoming the popular location for specialized instruction spaces that feature high-end computing, digital visualization, and gaming, among other offerings. Figure 2.16 illustrates several examples of these types of spaces. One reason for this growing popularity is the centrality of the library within the campus, but—maybe more importantly—the library represents neutral space that is not owned or controlled by any specific department. Economics also plays a part; for instance, it is more cost effective to build one visualization lab in the library that can be shared by all rather than several located in individual departments, schools, or colleges throughout the campus.

These technologically advanced classrooms and teaching spaces require skill and experience to operate effectively. Library staff and faculty must often teach and explain how to use these spaces, requiring a new set of skills and training beyond traditional services. This, in turn, can result in the re-designation of tasks and roles, and requires changes in the design of spaces that house traditional library functions.

Public libraries also are reimagining how to better meet the needs of communities they serve. This often leads to mission-specific teaching spaces such as early childhood literacy spaces, young adult hangout or homework spaces, active creation spaces (makerspaces), and even culinary teaching kitchens.

INHIBITORS

Rapidly evolving technologies require constant hardware and software upgrades. It seems that every year there is pressure to trade in a relatively new cell phone for the latest model or get a new television with a higher high-definition image. Books have been written on the importance for individuals, leaders, and businesses to adapt to change. The mantra "Change or die" is well known, and users expect libraries to keep pace. The fact is that change is constant and everywhere, and the notion that libraries are changing is indisputable. Because of this, it is helpful to understand the obstacles inherent in modern library design that inhibit libraries' ability to adapt to change. Obstacles to adaptability are known as *inhibitors of change*.

Libraries Are Inherently Inflexible

In the past, libraries were designed as bulwarks to house and protect precious materials. They were envisioned as vaults to store the printed word for centuries into the future and to accommodate limited growth of the collections. The conventional thinking of that time could never have imagined digital resources, online databases, downloadable and streaming content, and cloud-based computing. The result was library architecture designed to be permanent and inflexible. In fact, planners were so confident in the longevity of print materials that many early and midcentury libraries utilized the book stacks as structural support for elevated floors.

This inherent inflexibility is a huge inhibitor to libraries' ability to accommodate rapid change, not only in technology but also in how services are provided and how users access them. With the advent of computers and myriad handheld devices, it is common to see library users sitting on the floor, huddled around power outlets, while chairs remain empty elsewhere in the library. In these instances, the building's infrastructure is not easily adaptable to the demand for power at every seat.

Remedy: Adaptability

Figure 2.17. (a) Examples of construction that allow flexibility at Stanford University's d.school. (b) These images from a raised-floor installation in a library show ductwork and cabling installed on the floor rather than overhead in the ceiling plenum.

Libraries designed with hard walls and fixed locations for specific functions (service desk, office staff, book stacks, reading space, newspaper space, and so on) must be reconfigured with open floor plans and furniture that is both flexible and movable. Information desks on wheels are much easier to relocate when it comes time to rethink the use of space in the library. Similarly, offices without walls are easier to relocate and, as workers have found, can facilitate collaboration. Using furniture to define space and zones allows users and staff alike to rearrange space within the library.

Raised-floor systems that allow power and data receptacle locations to be moved and relocated as furniture arrangements change over time offer tremendous flexibility. In renovations, low-profile (3 inches or less) raised-floor systems can be added over existing concrete slabs fairly easily, with careful consideration given to existing door and stair locations. In new libraries or additions to existing structures, the incorporation of underfloor air distribution (UFAD) systems within the raised floor offer even more flexibility because they allow for the adjustment of HVAC grille locations. This type of system is generally more sustainable and energy efficient than a typical overhead forced air system.

Libraries Are Inherently Furniture Intensive

Libraries are more furniture driven than most other buildings. Many buildings can be designed without much thought given to the contents inside; however, libraries must be designed with full consideration given to their contents. Architects refer to libraries' contents as FF&E, which stands for fixtures, furnishings, and equipment. FF&E are the things that would fall out of the building if the roof were removed and the building turned upside down.

Most existing libraries contain FF&E that were installed the day it opened. This means the majority of the furniture and shelving in most libraries is decades old, outdated, and uncomfortable. As technology evolved and was introduced into the library, existing furniture was adapted, often with unattractive and inefficient results. This, combined with the natural ebb and flow of the collections and the introduction of new information media, means FF&E were constantly rearranged and repurposed. Over time, this resulted in a piecemeal approach to furniture layout. When this cycle is compounded over many years through incremental adjustments to the FF&E, libraries can become very inefficient and even nonfunctional without realizing it.

Remedy: Flexible Furniture

Figure 2.18. Mobile shelving units are growing in popularity. While they are more expensive, many libraries are utilizing them throughout their facilities, along with other mobile furniture that can be easily rearranged by users.

In order to avoid repeating history, it is important to invest in FF&E that are flexible and mobile. Figure 2.18 is an example of shelving made mobile through the use of casters. Furniture that is easily reconfigured and rearranged will make the incremental moves that are inevitable throughout the life of the library easier, thus allowing the library to remain efficient to accommodate growth and change.

Flexibility for users to rearrange furniture on their own is also important for spaces such as meeting rooms and collaboration areas. This can save the staff time and effort because they will not have to set up rooms.

Libraries Are Undersized

In the past, academic libraries were planned and sized based on ratios of square feet (SF) per full-time equivalent students (FTEs), and public libraries were sized based on population projections for a given service area. This was a formulaic approach based on a twenty-year growth projection for the communities they served. At the time, twenty years seemed like an eternity and basing size on such projections seemed to provide more space than would ever be needed. Technically, these formulas accommodated some future growth, but only at the pace and in the format (print-based) collected at the time. After many decades, however, library staff and services expanded, new information media were introduced, and computers were added, forcing more resources into the original, now undersized design.

Usually, these libraries were located in the heart of their campuses and communities, without consideration or accommodation for future expansion. As the campuses and communities grew up around these libraries, they became landlocked and outdated sooner than ever imagined.

Remedy #1: Relocation/Consolidation/ Cooperation

Figure 2.19. Off-site repositories utilizing (a) high-bay storage, (b) compact shelving for archives and special collections, and (c) traditional shelving that was removed from the main library

When an existing library cannot be replaced or expanded, a Road Map can illuminate a path to a renovated library that is more efficient and functional, with more capacity for the elements it currently lacks. Creating a "new" library within an existing building footprint that cannot be expanded means that something will have to move.

Most libraries begin by consolidating services and departments that are scattered throughout the facility to maximize efficiency and eliminate redundancies and inefficiencies that are wasting precious space. In almost every case, libraries are consolidating the footprint of low-use print materials into more efficient shelving systems or relocating lesser used items in separate, off-site storage facilities. Figure 2.19 illustrates three academic library repositories utilizing different storage strategies. Additionally, some libraries have identified several back-end operations such as technical services functions, preservation/conservation, digitizing, and administration that do not require direct access to the public and can be relocated away from the main library location.

Libraries have also adopted cooperative strategies for collection management and long-term print storage. In some academic library consortia, collections specialists have worked together to write print collection policies focused on shared responsibility for subject disciplines. For example, College A might focus on acquiring in philosophy and religion, while College B acquires in sociology and psychology. College C could then address acquisitions in chemistry and physics, with the result that the single copy of a book is shared among the participating libraries, eliminating the need for all three to place it in their collections. Over time, and using many academic disciplines, the result is fewer print books in the collection of individual libraries and more sharing of print resources, with concomitant reduction in shelving needs. This shared copy approach can also be applied to legacy print collections in library consortia, where participating academic libraries agree to keep materials in certain disciplines and the others discard them, with the remaining materials shared among consortium members. A similar approach can be used when libraries share a storage facility to house low-use materials; instead of all the libraries placing copies of the same title into the storage facility, one copy is selected that is then shared by member institutions. Public libraries are also cooperating to save space in these ways, and the space that is saved can be significant.

Approaches like these are relieving pressure on undersized libraries and freeing up space within them that can be repurposed for new and more pressing needs. This involves planning and cooperation among functional units, but can yield large amounts of space without a building expansion.

Remedy #2: Workflow Efficiency/Flexibility

Figure 2.20. In many libraries, efficient processes and workflows are hindered by overcrowded and disorganized workspaces.

In an environment where more than 90 percent of material budgets have shifted from print-based materials to electronic resources used for scholarship and information, the remaining staff support areas designed originally for processing and supporting print collections have become disorganized and inefficient (see figure 2.20). Compounded by decades of unplanned growth, these existing spaces should be redesigned to create new efficiencies and save space through streamlined processes, reorganized staff configurations, and redesigned workflows to increase efficiency.

Libraries Are Financially Challenged

Needless to say, it is difficult and expensive for libraries to continuously procure new FF&E and infrastructure for evolving technologies and services. It may even be harder to fund renovations and construct additions to accommodate ever-increasing programs and offerings to serve their communities. Even when a library's need is evident and recognized, it might struggle for funding and is often competing with other important community or institutional needs, interests, and priorities that take precedence.

Additionally, pressures on institutional funding sources in many cases have resulted in cutbacks, delayed or deferred projects, and even suspension of capital spending. Both public and academic institutions are being forced to take a second, closer look to ensure their libraries are achieving their best and highest use. In response to systemic budget challenges and economic pressures, one administrator who oversees capital improvements for all the academic and public libraries in his state said:

> In this new environment, the major challenge is not building capacity; it is first to ensure the existing capacity is used as efficiently and effectively as possible. Accordingly, we must ensure that we are utilizing our entire space well before new buildings are approved. (Hank Huckaby, Chancellor, University System of Georgia)

This does not mean there are not undersized libraries out there that need more space. But it is a call for a close examination of how all the available space is being used before embarking on the path to renovate or build additional space with scarce financial resources.

TRADITIONAL MASTER PLANNING VERSUS THE ROAD MAP APPROACH

TRADITIONAL MASTER PLAN

ROAD MAP APPROACH

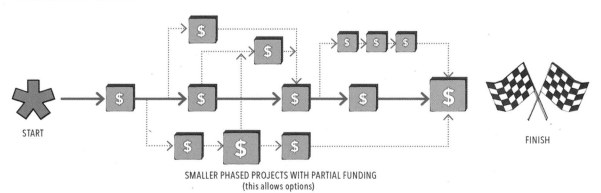

Figure 2.21. Traditional master plan versus Road Map approach

A traditional library master plan describes the current condition (the starting point) and a final destination (the end point). Master plans are great and useful tools that articulate an ultimate vision and unite stakeholders. However, traditional master plans usually come with such exorbitant price tags, rigidity, and lengthy implementation periods that they are abandoned or become antiquated before the full vision is realized—resulting in squandered effort, hope, and excitement.

Economic pressures on institutional funding, as mentioned earlier, exacerbate the problem, resulting in cutbacks, delays, or deferred projects and forcing public and private institutions to take a closer look to ensure their facilities are achieving their best and highest use. When an institution is simply trying to survive, it becomes increasingly difficult to see opportunities for progress and optimization, and even master plans can seem too esoteric to invest the time and money needed to develop.

Instead of just making do, the Road Map approach to master planning demonstrates how to make the most of a space and increase its capacity, efficiency, and functionality.

Yogi Berra once said, "If you don't know where you are going, you'll end up someplace else." The witty baseball guru's play on the old adage that "any road will get you there" explains why the Road Map has become an effective alternative to traditional master plans for library planning.

As an alternative planning method, the Road Map not only defines the destination but provides a multitude of options to get there with inherent flexibility, prioritized milestones, and enumerated phased implementation steps. Both the Road Map approach and the traditional master plan begin with a library in need and finish with a transformative vision, but the Road Map offers a more flexible approach.

A traditional master plan customarily offers a transformative vision whose execution is contingent on funding the entire program. However, in difficult economic conditions, projects with high budgets sometimes have a lower chance for implementation. If not dead on arrival due to an ambitious cost that may take years to fund, these master plans are often shelved and collect dust while current needs remain unmet.

By comparison, the Road Map outlines incremental and prioritized steps to achieve the transformative vision, also offering an opportunity to extract elements or areas as candidates for expedited individual projects with naming rights and recognition of generous donors. The flexibility of this planning method also adapts more readily to changing circumstances than a traditional master plan (see figure 2.22).

One regional public library director described her experience this way:

> The architect reimagined our library space in a way that none of us had ever thought of, and is exactly what we needed! The Road Map they provided, which detailed ways we could do the work in independent phases, turned out to be incredibly useful when we had an unexpected chance to do some work ahead of the major renovation. Since we already had a plan in place, we were able to jump on the opportunity. (Geri Lynn Mullis, Director, Marshes of Glynn Libraries)

THE ROAD MAP AND TRADITIONAL MASTER PLANNING

During the mid-1990s, while I was employed at a large academic library, a well-known planning firm was retained to provide a detailed renovation proposal for the present structure of 350,000 sq. ft. The process took about nine months and resulted in a detailed report printed on paper. It was probably three inches thick and included multiple examples of floor plans, furniture layouts, equipment recommendations, and visible space upgrades in the form of ceremonial entrances, vistas, and promenades. However, while the planners carefully considered the library user, the key focus was the traditional library setting, with an emphasis on solitary study in the form of individual study carrels in the stacks and classrooms for teaching bibliographical instruction. The planning process appeared to have revolved around users as groups rather than individuals. For example, there was a recommendation for a graduate (student) reading room, a humanities reading room, a social sciences reading room, etc. In describing these spaces, planners mentioned sacred space, sightlines, linearity, and symmetry. But they said nothing about flexible space, reconfigurable furniture, changing forms of student learning, and the recently embraced Internet and how it might change things.

The phasing approach was simple: first, close one floor of the library and renovate, then repeat until all the floors were finished. Any consideration for flexibility was confined to a section designated *additive alternate* (add-alt, in planning terms) that would provide for additional features, space use, or a higher level of design complexity should funding be available. This was less about flexibility and more about providing some choice for the end user to determine what features and design options would best match available funding. It was expected that the project cost would hinge on these factors and not on phasing of the work. The project was priced as a single cost, with a few add-alts included to provide for choices among library administrators. What the planners presented was a wonderful vision for a marvelous structure, but one that would be completely out of date within only a few years and obsolete within a single decade. In any event, funding issues rendered the point moot and the plan was never put into place. The amount of money required to do the complete renovation was in the millions of dollars, and this seemed insurmountable for those in control of the purse strings.

This traditional master plan exemplifies the all-or-nothing approach. In contrast, the new Road Map process is more efficient and effective for the following reasons:

- Individual library users and their needs are key in considering space planning.

- Library space is not considered static, and will in fact be expected to change over both the short and the long term.

- Technology is a primary driver, even when planning while not knowing completely what the next new library technology might be.

- Phasing breaks the renovation project into smaller projects that can be priced for cost and fund-raising purposes, allowing discrete parts of a given project to proceed even before all project funding is identified.

–Eric Shoaf, MLS, MPA

Dean of the Library
Queens University of Charlotte

Figure 2.22. The Road Map and traditional master planning

BENEFITS OF THE ROAD MAP APPROACH

Q: How do you eat an elephant?
A: One bite at a time.

As mentioned above, the primary distinction between a traditional master plan and the Road Map approach is the incorporation of a phased implementation strategy and the inherent flexibility it offers. This is in fact one of the most beneficial aspects of the Road Map approach.

Road Maps Offer Flexibility and Phased Implementation

A traditional master plan may seem like an elephant of a project. The Road Map approach breaks it down into smaller segments that can be executed and funded as separate, smaller projects over a longer period of time and as opportunities arise. A traditional master plan, for instance, may require several years to identify and acquire the total funding for the project. The Road Map approach enables a library to begin and execute initial phases during that same period as smaller projects based on funding sources that become available. In the traditional master plan, nothing happens for the first several years; with a Road Map, change begins sooner. This fuels another benefit—it creates hope. Speaking of this benefit, one librarian stated:

> Incorporating knowledge of trends in library design combined with assessment data from students, faculty, and staff, the architect, working with me and my staff, developed a Road Map that outlined incremental changes that led to a desired outcome to meet our needs. Since then, I use the Road Map every week to guide our efforts in renovation, to formulate budget requests, and to support service decisions. The Road Map has been presented to the university's administration and the feedback has been very positive.
>
> The results happened quickly, and were enjoyed by the campus immediately. The administration of the institution was able to hear positive feedback and use the library as a showcase for recruitment. The beauty of our incremental plan was that I was always prepared for opportunities to upgrade the facility when the institution solicited proposals for expenditure of end-of-year funds. The plan also provided some protection for space overreach because there were utilization plans in place. The incremental implementation provided a road map or "playbook" to advance the library's goals, based on needs assessment and feedback from library users. (Kay Wall, Dean of Libraries [Retired], Clemson University)

Road Maps Create Hope

> My staff was energized by the process and excited by the results. (Laura Davidson, Dean of Library Information Services, Meredith College)

The process of developing a Road Map is inclusive, collaborative, and iterative, and as things begin to happen, excitement and enthusiasm grows. When library administrators, staff, and faculty come together to identify, define, and address current deficiencies and articulate how the library should meet users' needs moving forward, a future vision develops. The process leading to the vision is often as unifying as the vision itself.

In the Road Map planning process, participants can hear the rationale behind the proposed changes and engage in conversations that drive critical decisions. Their participation builds consensus and fosters a sense of ownership and authorship for the vision. Consensus leads to a unified group, and a unified group that has developed a vision and believes it to be attainable will be more willing to make it happen. Moving forward, everyone understands the reasons behind the initial work, phases, and steps that must occur. As tasks are completed and checked off the list, momentum is gained. It is powerful to see the results of positive change in an environment where it was once assumed that change was unaffordable or impossible or so far into the future it would never happen. Two librarians expressed it this way:

> Perhaps the most satisfying aspect of this project was the process. . . . [T]his high-level open engagement with the entire library led to a plan that is both substantively outstanding and universally embraced and accepted (very important to its implementation). As evidence of its high level of acceptance, the staff gave the architect an impromptu standing ovation upon his library-wide public presentation/review of the final plan. As dean, I'm still waiting for such a staff accolade when presenting ideas. (Dana Sally, Dean of Libraries [Retired], Western Carolina University)

> The final drawings provided by the architect are proudly displayed on the wall adjacent to the office of the dean of library services. We are taking a staged approach to the renovation and every change has produced a boost in morale and compliments from faculty and students. (S. David Mash, PhD, Vice President for Academic Affairs and Former Dean of Library Services, Lander University)

Road Maps Allow for Adjustments along the Way

There is probably not a librarian on earth who would not take the entire sum needed to completely execute the library's master plan if given the option, nor is there an architect who would recommend against that choice. With that said, however, in the more common circumstance—when funding takes time to identify or comes in through incremental budgeting or gifts—the longer time it takes to complete the final vision does have an upside: It allows for adjustments to be integrated into the unfinished portion of the Road Map as new requirements, services, and technologies arise.

Obviously, the upside to having all the funding at one time and moving forward with the entire project is that the renovation happens quickly and all the space is improved at the same time. If there is a downside, it is that the construction process happens relatively quickly and the end result is a snapshot of what a new library should look like in that moment; if not planned correctly, that library may become a time capsule of what was considered conventional library design at that time—which is often the problem with the existing library.

The Road Map approach allows for new technologies, services, thoughts on collection management strategies and spaces, and so on to be integrated throughout the course of the library's transformation. It also allows for experimentation and prototyping on a small scale to see whether certain technologies, FF&E arrangements, and approaches work as intended and are accepted by users before they are implemented throughout the library at a significant cost.

> Technology has been and will continue to be a big driver in library renovation. Disruptive technology has the potential to alter the best master planning, so flexibility in design and function should always be considered. There has to be an acknowledgement somewhere in the process that you can't get all of the technology possibilities "right" because it changes so rapidly.
>
> The library's Road Map plan provided realistic opportunities for change where an "all at once" Master Plan would have taken years to be funded. The intervening years between major facility capital projects are long periods of living with undesirable work and study space. During those times, the opportunity for the library to reflect a welcoming learning environment is practically nonexistent. As a result, students typically do not view their library experience as a positive one. (Kay Wall, Dean of Libraries [Retired], Clemson University)

Road Maps Demonstrate Leadership

It is one thing to ask for new or additional space and updated technology and get it, but it is another to *not* receive what was requested and move forward anyway. A Road Map equips a librarian to do just that, through good stewardship of valuable and scarce resources. Furthermore, when a librarian can show stakeholders a Road Map that utilizes the existing facility to its best and highest use, it is easier and more credible to defend and substantiate requests for increased funding and improved facilities. When a librarian's request for funds is less than the millions a new or completely renovated facility would cost, that demonstrates leadership.

Road Maps Demonstrate Sustainability

Too often we think sustainable design is applicable only to new buildings that incorporate energy-saving strategies, reduce the consumption of water, utilize recycled and renewable materials, or achieve some level of a green rating system; however, it can be argued that the most sustainable building is the one that is not built at all. By extending the life and usefulness of an existing facility, the consumption of valuable energy and resources is deferred.

CHALLENGES TO THE ROAD MAP APPROACH

While the benefits are compelling and seem obvious to those who experience the need for change on a daily basis, implementing a Road Map can expose and present challenges that have to be overcome. Below are some of the challenges encountered by librarians who have completed successful Road Maps of their own.

Obtaining Internal Buy-In

It is essential that library leadership be aligned in agreement on the need to embark on the development of a Road Map. This does not mean that everyone will initially agree as to what should be done or what the strategic priorities should be; however, if everyone is committed to fully participating, communicating honestly, and acting on what is best for the community they serve, the Road Map will be a success that everyone can rally around as incremental steps are initiated.

> Because master planning requires a huge commitment of time and resources from all library staff, the first challenge was to get their "buy-in," or permission. Without this internal commitment and motivation, master

planning becomes an extremely arduous undertaking—one that might be doomed to failure. This "internal" permission can involve a long period of discourse in which all get to contribute to setting library mission priorities and gaining an understanding of how space design is organically connected to successfully meeting the agreed-upon priorities. (Dana Sally, Dean of Libraries [Retired], Western Carolina University)

Convincing Decision Makers

Convincing those outside the library to provide authorization, permission, or funding to embark on a Road Map is often the first and most formidable challenge. A compelling case for proceeding can be made effectively by appealing to the broader institutional mission and demonstrating the needs of the library users. In every case, presenting a unified front and demonstrating consensus among library leadership is essential in making the case to those outside the library.

> Once you have staff buy-in, then developing a motivational narrative for external audiences becomes a library-wide priority and all are embracing the same consistent story, or need, for master planning. In the case of our library, this began with a rather long process of developing a library strategic plan that was vetted both internally and externally on campus, engaging all affected campus constituents: students, faculty, and campus administration.
>
> In addition, the library had also been collecting user satisfaction data via the LibQual survey for a number of years that revealed certain "satisfaction gaps" were related to both library services and library building use. Follow-up exploration of this survey allowed us to demonstrate that specific changes were needed and being called for. In other words, we tied needed changes to the core mission of the institution: supporting the educational needs of students and faculty.
>
> Also for three consecutive years, I collected feedback from brand-new university faculty during their library orientation. Most of these faculty were coming from PhD programs at other universities—with very good libraries—and had entered our library for the very first time. I simply asked them for their very first impressions of the building upon entering it. This feedback was very revealing of the fact that we had some unique and pressing space design challenges. (Dana Sally, Dean of Libraries [Retired], Western Carolina University)

Those Resistant to Change

Almost without exception, there will be change-resistant individuals within the library or institution who are comfortable with the status quo. Sometimes these individuals perceive change as something requiring additional work; in other instances they are nostalgic for libraries of old. In rare instances, those who had a hand in planning or renovating the current space are still involved and see further change as an indictment of their past efforts. It is important to try to understand the motivations and perspectives driving this resistance to change so these individuals can be brought on board to the greatest extent possible.

> One major challenge to our Road Map efforts was those who lacked vision and were resistant to change. What I encountered were individuals who didn't have much experience in thinking about library facilities, were deeply entrenched as "long timers" in ways things had always been done and who, possibly, were not exposed to other places that operated differently. (Kay Wall, Dean of Libraries [Retired], Clemson University)

Everyone's an Expert

Those in positions of authority did not usually get there from a lack of confidence or opinions. As alternatives and options for the library are discussed and considered, individuals will weigh in with their thoughts and ideas. Sometimes these are fresh and insightful, but other times they can be completely off-base and counterproductive to the direction the library needs to be heading. Receiving this input without implementing it—while communicating respect and appreciation—can be tricky and requires careful navigation of ego and politics.

> There will be those outside the library who know nothing about library operations and functions who are more than happy to tell you what to do. (Kay Wall, Dean of Libraries [Retired], Clemson University)

Who Not to Include

While participation and involvement in the Road Map process should be wide and inclusive, not everyone can participate and be involved in every decision. Knowing where to draw the line regarding who is integral to the decision-making process and who is not can be difficult.

> One challenge was how to deal with the realization that not everyone in a large staff can be involved in the Road Map process. While everyone's input and ideas were welcomed, not everyone could be at the table for every decision. (Kay Wall, Dean of Libraries [Retired], Clemson University)

Competing Interests

Some individuals, administrators, or facility personnel may not see the library's needs as the highest priority. Building alliances with advocates outside the library is crucial to achieving success.

> The biggest hurdle was persuading our facilities managers that developing a Road Map as a part of our review process would not affect their ability to manage the campus as a whole. (Laura Davidson, Dean of Library Information Services, Meredith College)

Funding the Implementation

Identifying funding for the Road Map—and more importantly, its implementation—is possibly the most common challenge encountered.

> Funding for carrying out the Road Map remains a challenge. At the outset of our capital campaign, I had great hopes we would find a donor to support the changes but that hasn't happened. (Laura Davidson, Dean of Library Information Services, Meredith College)

CONCLUSION

Master planning a library makes sense and is an invaluable tool to provide a framework that informs future planning and progress leading to a final vision. When funding is not available for wholesale renovation or construction of a new building, the Road Map offers many benefits over the traditional library master planning approach. It offers a flexible plan that allows for phased implementation in smaller, more affordable steps. It creates hope, demonstrates leadership, and exhibits a commitment to sustainability.

Creating a Road Map for an existing library can breathe new life into an antiquated facility. By maximizing a library's efficiency, functionality, and capacity through an effective, well-thought-out Road Map, an existing library with no room for growth and expansion becomes a library with increased space for programs and services that serve its community.

It sounds too good to be true, but in many cases libraries have achieved significant increases in needed furniture and space without having to add a single square foot of new space. Often we become inoculated to the environment around us and fail to see opportunities that are obvious to others. Sometimes people are so invested in planning decisions of the past that they are unable to see the need to change, adapt, and adjust to new circumstances. In other cases, they become so comfortable with the current arrangement that the thought of wholesale change is just too daunting. The Road Map approach invites creative thinking that leads to the transformation of existing libraries—large or small, public or academic.

The Road Map approach can demonstrate good stewardship of current space and strengthen the argument for meaningful renovations that address true needs. The process informs how to best utilize existing FF&E and maximize the inflexible bunkers of the past into relevant libraries that accommodate growth, services, and technologies, now and into the future.

3

PROCESS

The process employed in the creation of a Road Map is fluid and iterative. It is essential for librarians, staff, stakeholders, and users to take an active role in the creation of the ultimate vision for library space use. The goal is to create a library that will effectively and flexibly accommodate activities and programs that the community or campus needs; there is no way to understand what this looks like unless those who live in that world are engaged in the process. The better the input, the more reliable the output.

Beginning with an understanding of the existing conditions, the process of creating a Road Map ends with a vision of the final destination. The process is comprised of the following six steps:

Step 1: Assess/analyze   Step 4: Design/plan
Step 2: Engage/listen   Step 5: Phasing/strategize
Step 3: Program/define   Step 6: Estimate/budget

SIX STEPS TO A ROAD MAP

01
ASSESS | *analyze*

02
ENGAGE | *listen*

03
PROGRAM | *define*

04
DESIGN | *plan*

05
PHASING | *strategize*

06
ESTIMATE | *budget*

Figure 3.1. Six steps to a Road Map

STEP I: ASSESS/ANALYZE

You can't know where you are going until you know where you have been.

—James Baldwin

Before planning any trip, it is necessary to understand where it begins. When embarking on a Road Map, the place to begin is with the library itself. By understanding what works and what does not, planners gain insight into what the library's potential is and which issues rank highest on the list of items to be addressed in the future vision. Gaining a holistic understanding of existing conditions requires a multifaceted, global analysis and thorough examination of the existing library facility, the surrounding context, and the internal processes it contains (or does not support). Planners will familiarize themselves with the existing conditions, building systems, furniture, documentation, studies, reports, and any current drawings or plans that may be available to glean insight and perspective on the current layout and condition of the library. As a result of the existing facility assessment phase, a set of current floor plans and furniture layouts are created and used as a basis for the Road Map.

This process of assessment begins with, but is not limited to, close examination of the following issues.

Surrounding Context

The immediate surrounding site/campus context should be reviewed to understand influences and opportunities as well as restricting factors that affect the current and future potential of the library facility. Issues such as vehicular and pedestrian circulation routes, building entry and loading locations, solar orientation, potential expansion space, and overall aesthetic and visibility considerations can impact how the Road Map develops. Information to review may include the following.

Previously Published Visionary Documents

Planners should review campus or community master plans, strategic plans, and mission and vision statements. Any documents that may inform current planning considerations or reveal previously discovered issues to address in the current planning effort should be included.

Local Zoning and Planning Ordinances

Zoning and planning ordinances often specify minimum parking requirements and building area and height limitations, which can influence the expansion capabilities of a specific library on a specific site.

Existing Facility

Assessing the existing facility requires examination of not only the physical characteristics of the building but also the systems, furniture, and processes that it contains. When developing a Road Map, it is important to identify elements within the building that are critical to the existing building systems and would be costly to modify, such as electrical panel, mechanical rooms, and toilet locations, as well as shortcomings that should be corrected. Issues to be examined may include the following.

Current Building Codes

Because Road Maps often involve some interior renovations, it is important to understand where the existing building may fall short of current building codes. Often, these codes have stricter requirements than they did when the building was constructed, and if the scope of the renovations is extensive enough, code upgrades could be required. In addition to life safety issues, consideration must be given to increased requirements of current energy codes. Upgrading an existing facility's systems can be expensive, and thoughtful consideration should be given to include these potential costs in the estimates that are provided in the final report.

Evaluation of Current Systems

To determine if current systems fall short of codes, they have to be evaluated with regard to energy performance. Additionally, anecdotal evidence almost always indicates underperformance with regard to comfort or reliability that must also be taken into account. It is important to understand how current systems are zoned and how HVAC is distributed so that development of phasing plans can take this into consideration as portions of the library are identified for isolation and renovation. Electrical distribution and capacity should be evaluated to understand the increase in electrical capacity required for current technologies and audiovisual resources. This will also represent an additional cost that must be factored into Road Map cost estimates.

Structural Capacity

It is important to determine whether the structural capacity of the existing structure and floors meets current seismic requirements and whether it allows for rearranging library shelving and other heavy equipment. This can have a tremendous impact on how and where physical collections may be located in the Road Map.

Accessibility Requirements

Libraries constructed prior to 1990 often fall short of ADA and other accessibility code requirements. The Road Map should address these shortcomings and include any required upgrades into cost estimates that are included in the final report.

Deferred Maintenance Issues

Often, the Road Map planning process identifies deferred maintenance that is negatively impacting the library. As the scope of the Road Map is considered, remediation of these issues should be accounted for in cost estimates.

Presence of Hazardous Materials

In older facilities, environmental studies should be performed to identify the possibility of existing hazardous materials such as asbestos or lead paint. If these materials are present, then cost estimates for removal should be included in the Road Map.

Interior/Environmental Qualities

Not to be confused with sustainability issues and efforts, this category focusing on interior/environmental qualities takes into consideration the quality of the library space and includes issues such as lighting, character, views to the exterior, daylight, acoustics, and so on. Attention should be given to how the building enhances (or does not enhance) the experience of the users and how it can be improved.

Internal Processes

Internal processes include work procedures and processes, and their impact on the library's mission to those it serves and the institution it supports. The question "Does the library work?" should be evaluated from the viewpoint of both the user and library staff. Furthermore, the question must be evaluated on different functional levels, including workflows, technologies, processes, collections, and so on. The library may work well in some areas but not in others. Anecdotal evidence and on-site observations will add much insight to this complicated and layered assessment. Areas to consider include the following.

Fixtures, Furnishings, and Equipment Review

Usually, the existing furniture in a library was installed the day it opened, and only in rare cases has it been replaced or upgraded. If the furniture is replaced after the grand opening, it often happens in a piecemeal fashion in response to limited renovations. When assessing the functionality of a library, the furniture must be examined to determine if it has any remaining life left, and if so, whether it can be utilized in a reenvisioned space. This process typically involves creating a detailed inventory of the existing furniture and plans that document the current furniture arrangement. After conceptual plans are developed, the new furniture arrangements and quantities are compared with the existing ones, and through a comparative analysis a budget for the new furniture is established. This budget information, in turn, is incorporated into the estimates included in the Road Map.

Collection Management Evaluation

How a library addresses the legacy print collection and responds to the impact of digital media on the acquisition of print materials can have a tremendous impact on opportunities for reenvisioning existing space. Conversations may include trends and anticipated growth or reductions to be made in print collections and what, if any, deaccessioning or weeding efforts will take place. Whatever collections remain will have to be stored in some fashion. Conversations about how and where this will take place are of primary importance. For academic libraries, in many instances serious consideration should be given to the strategy of an off-site storage repository and its impact on staffing, service, and space.

Special Collections and Archives

Special collections and archives have become marks of distinction for the institutions that own them. They are ever increasing in size and value, and are often irreplaceable. They require special environmental and security provisions. Where they will be located, accessed, displayed, and stored is an important strategic decision that can affect the location of other departments. Accommodation for large donations can have a tremendous impact on the space needs identified in the Road Map. Often the current state of these collections and work spaces is inadequate and puts materials at risk. It is important to define the scope and location of special collections since they will have an impact on the cost estimates that are included in the Road Map.

Functionality and Workflow Analysis

As the communities and institutions served by libraries grow, so does the staff and support needed to service them. Usually this means that staff and their support functions outgrow the spaces originally designed to house them, and this can result in fragmented departments or teams. The physical manifestation of this often results in an inefficient and ineffective arrangement that impacts a staff's sense of teamwork and morale. The Road Map should address how departments and materials should be repositioned to be more efficient and effective. The impact of technologies on workflows should also be taken into account. As user habits and library services evolve, points of staff interaction must evolve as well. Their locations and the services they provide will change; the Road Map should address these issues.

Partners and Tenants

Public and academic libraries alike are aligning themselves with partners inside and outside their organizations to better serve users and their communities. This can impact how library space is organized and allocated. Some partners are invited into the library on a temporary basis and need a designated place to land. In other cases, partners have a permanent presence in the library and space is thoughtfully designed for their specific purpose. Examples of partners for academic and public libraries alike that a Road Map might address include career services, counseling, information technology, broadcast communications, academic support, tutoring, writing center, cafés, classrooms, and so on.

01 ASSESS | analyze

DELIVERABLES

- Photo documentation of existing building conditions

- Existing floor and furniture plans

- Engineering narratives documenting existing system evaluations

- Any relevant previously published visionary documents

- Written reports enumerating:

  ◦ ADA shortcomings

  ◦ Deferred maintenance issues

  ◦ Presence of hazardous materials

  ◦ Additional relevant findings

Figure 3.2. 01 Assess/Analyze

STEP 2: ENGAGE/LISTEN

A   B   C

Figure 3.3. (a) A community meeting prior to the design of a new public library; (b) university visioning meeting with stakeholders from across campus to discuss ways the library can improve the student experience; (c) an engagement meeting of all the deans at a small private college to discuss how the library can improve the services offered to students in each of their areas of focus

Because it is critical for libraries to collaborate with partner organizations that share their mission to both identify community challenges and to seek methods and funding to resolve them, it is essential for libraries to host community conversations to address the unique needs of each community they serve. Using human-centered design will guide the approach for building facilities, providing services, allocating resources, and advancing the community. (Roberta Phillips, Planning and Projects Director, Richland Library)

A successful Road Map is one that has built consensus among all the stakeholders throughout its development and is accepted and embraced by those stakeholders. It reflects and responds effectively to the community or institution it serves. Achieving this requires involvement of many interested parties early and often in the engagement process. By engaging those who have a vested interest to glean their ideas, input, and perspective, the library will be able to meet their needs more effectively and achieve success in the planning process (see figure 3.3).

Every administrator, faculty and staff member, facilities personnel, student, and user has a unique perspective and set of criteria that define a successful library. Each may define this somewhat differently. For some it means being able to find a seat with available power; for others the technology or assistance offered has priority; another subset may be most interested in a facility that is efficient and easy to maintain. Although success means different things to different people, it does not mean that satisfying various space criteria is

a mutually exclusive proposition. In fact, the most successful Road Map is one that achieves the most goals for the most people without compromising the library's mission and vision.

The engagement phase utilizes tools and methods to collect input and perspective through the use of interviews, focus group discussions, surveys, and on-site observations. Figure 3.4 illustrates a matrix of groups to engage that will help to ensure the library casts a broad enough net when reaching out to its community for input.

Those outside the library staff, because of the departmental leadership, responded very well to the master plan and its portents for the future. The campus began a master planning activity at about the time the library had completed its plan and the library's plan was incorporated into the all-campus plan at the end of that process.

I firmly believe that the general enthusiastic reception of the library's plan was based on the fact that all important campus groups were included in the planning process from the beginning. The process was very broad-based and inclusive, starting with the campus administration and moving through student government, faculty senate, external support units housed in the library, the campus planning office, the university architect, and campus facilities management. As a former supervisor once remarked to me, "If you want me with you on the landing, make sure I'm with you on the takeoff." (Dana Sally, Dean of Libraries [Retired], Western Carolina University)

LIBRARY PERSONNEL*

PUBLIC LIBRARIES	Library Director Library Leadership Team Library Staff	Soliciting input from library staff members as part of the planning process is important because they interact with library users, technology, and the faculty on a daily basis. They have valuable knowledge and insight. Including them in the planning process is a substantiative way to increase the likelihood that they will support the final product.
ACADEMIC LIBRARIES	Library Director Library Leadership Team Library Staff	

INSTITUTIONAL LEADERSHIP*

PUBLIC LIBRARIES	County Administration County Councilmen Board/Trustee Members	Soliciting input from the institutional leadership is a strategic and important step, since these individuals often are decision makers regarding the library's funding. Furthermore, they can offer insight into their vision for institution and how they see the library supporting it. They will not always understand everything the library does in its service to users, but including them in the process is key to securing their ongoing support. These conversations can also help educate them on the current and future role of the library within the community or campus.
ACADEMIC LIBRARIES	College/University Leadership (i.e., President, Provost, etc.) Library Staff	

STAKEHOLDERS

PUBLIC LIBRARIES	Friends of the Library Organization Facilities/Maintenance Community Design Review Boards	Stakeholders are individuals, groups, and organizations that have a vested interest in the success of the library. They usually take care of the facility or offer financial support. Sometimes they have the power to approve the plans. Keeping them updated on the long-term vision and seeking their input early and often will communicate to them that their input is valued and appreciated.
ACADEMIC LIBRARIES	Campus Planning/Design Facilities/Maintenance	

USERS

PUBLIC LIBRARIES	Adults Young Adults/Teens Parents and Children Senior Citizens Others	The input from different user groups of the library is invaluable. It offers insight and a unique perspective regarding the services they use and value. Each user group will see the library differently through their own experiences. Their input should represent a fair and honest assessment by those who love and value the library. While user assessments can be harsh at times, the comments often come from a place of constructive criticism with the intent to make the library better.
ACADEMIC LIBRARIES	Faculty Students	

PARTNERSHIPS

PUBLIC LIBRARIES	Local Community Organizations Social Services Other County/Public Agencies	Talking with current and potential partners may help expand the library's understanding on how it is perceived by those on the outside. Often these groups think outside the box and offer ideas and/or services that can be strategic in redefining how the library can serve its community. Those partners who share the library's vision for serving its community can become strong library advocates to effect change and assist in the development of programs.
ACADEMIC LIBRARIES	Writing Center Academic Support Tutoring Other Partners	

* These individuals or committees are sometimes referred to as the *owner* elsewhere.

Figure 3.4. Engagement matrix

Why Is the Engagement Process Important?

Figure 3.5. Hearing from everyone in the community is essential.

Casting a broad net and making the engagement process inclusive will garner support and earn the library and its leadership credibility as the Road Map is revealed. The goal is to author a Road Map that is a win-win for as many stakeholders as possible and to minimize the number of those who are dissatisfied. To that end, it is important to be able to articulate the efforts made to solicit a multitude of input, perspectives, and opinions and to have an open and transparent process that allows everyone to voice their opinions. In the context of an inclusive engagement process, explanations can be given for the rationale that led to the decisions about what is ultimately included in the Road Map.

The following testimony does not speak directly to community engagement for a Road Map; however, it does speak to the power of engaging a community early and often in the planning process to gain community support and buy-in. The same is true when embarking on a Road Map to transform an existing facility. When bond

bill referendums for new libraries elsewhere in the region failed, this community was successful in getting one passed with over 70 percent support in the affirmative.

In 2014 the taxpayers of our county passed a $108.5 million bond initiative to build five new libraries, [to] renovate thirteen existing branches, and to upgrade technology throughout the library system. The success of this measure is directly linked to community engagement. Dozens of community meetings were held before the vote and hundreds of conversations took place with stakeholders, thought leaders, and community members. Since the passage of the vote, the library staff has continued to engage our community in the process, presenting design milestones and sharing updates. Community engagement is crucial for libraries in all that we do, as our branches belong to our citizens and they should represent a shared vision. (Nicolle Ingui Davies, Executive Director, Charleston County Public Library)

What Does the Engagement Process Entail?

Engagement meetings are discovery exercises that explore people's ideas, experiences, and opinions about how and what the library can do or be to remain relevant to the individuals and communities it serves. During these meetings, attendees are encouraged to share their thoughts, ask questions, and communicate what they feel is important and should be considered. These meetings are usually facilitated by the consultant hired to author the Road Map, with someone designated to take notes and document what is shared. A library representative is almost always present to answer specific questions that may come up, but at other times a representative may elect not to attend if concerned his or her presence may hinder openness and honest dialogue.

I think it is incredibly important that library staff feel that the architect leading the planning process has heard and understood their concerns about their workflows. I also think it is good to receive community input and have the institutional leadership feel that community needs are being considered in the development of the plans, not just library employee ideas. (Laura Davidson, Dean of Library Information Services, Meredith College)

Through observation and regular interactions with students, it was clear that our perceptions about their library needs were incongruent, and their needs were a major driver in changes. So, while changes in spaces to accommodate new/different resource needs for students were important, it was equally important to listen to students about what was important to them. The things they valued typically had nothing to do with the traditional values the library was attempting to impart to the students. (Kay Wall, Dean of Libraries [Retired], Clemson University)

A Typical Engagement Meeting Outline

The agenda for engagement meetings is fairly simple and follows an outline similar to the one below:

1. Introductions
2. Process, Project, and Purpose
3. Optional 5- to 10-Minute Presentation
4. Community Conversation
5. Wrap-Up
6. Participatory Exercise

Introductions

Introductions are usually handled by the consultant or library representative. If the group is small, it is good to have everyone introduce themselves and share with the group their interest in and use of the library. If the group is large and individual introductions would take too long, it is fine to introduce library and programming personnel and recognize dignitaries, asking attendees to introduce themselves when they speak.

Process, Project, and Purpose

An overview of the process and where the project is on the timeline is usually spelled out by the consultant or library representative to set the context for the meeting. The consultant or representative then explains that the purpose of the meeting is to provide a forum for the library to hear and understand everyone's thoughts, ideas, concerns, and so on, and that their comments will be taken into consideration as the Road Map process begins. If this is an open meeting, sufficient effort should be made to give adequate notice to the community.

Optional 5- to 10-Minute Presentation

Sometimes it is helpful for the consultant to give a brief overview of the Road Map process to help attendees understand the purpose of the meeting. If the meeting is to seek innovative thinking, sometimes a short presentation that illustrates case studies that demonstrate out-of-the-box approaches used elsewhere can help prime the pump for ideas that challenge the current paradigm. Other audiences may not understand why libraries are even needed or why they are changing. In those cases, a short explanation of current library trends may help educate attendees on the evolution taking place with libraries worldwide. In any event, the decision to present or not should be driven on what will most benefit the audience and what will best help solicit the input needed for a successful Road Map.

Community Conversation

The consultant should take the lead and facilitate the conversation but should not dominate it. He or she should avoid making assertions or drawing conclusions. Remember, the purpose of the engagement process is to draw input from the attendees to better understand what they think, feel, want, and need. The consultant should be a facilitator, not a lecturer.

One of the most effective ways to draw out people's thoughts and solicit ideas is to use a series of questions to spur and extend conversation. Questions should be thoughtful and not answerable with a simple yes or no response. They should be crafted to elicit opinions and insight to better illuminate how participants feel the "new" facility can best support their individual and community needs. Questions may include, but are not limited to:

- What about the existing library is most appealing?
- How do you primarily use the library?
- What do you wish the library offered that it doesn't?
- What do you love about the current library that should not be lost in the process of design or renovation?
- What do you feel the library needs more/less of?
- What are the weaknesses of the existing library that should be addressed in a new design?
- If you're not a current library user, what about a new library would make you begin using it?

When an answer is given in response to a question like one of those listed above, the facilitator should ask the person answering to elaborate. The facilitator might also ask the larger group to comment on what was said in case others see the issue differently. Either way, this will provide more insight and often reveal the underlying reasons behind the answer and associated comments. Below is an example of how a facilitator's response to an answer can extend a conversation to gain additional, valuable information:

Facilitator: What about the current library is most appealing?

Attendee: I like the comfortable chairs.

Facilitator: Okay, thanks.

In this exchange, the facilitator and the library did not learn very much useful information. A better approach might look like this:

Facilitator: What about the current library is most appealing?

Attendee: I like the comfortable chairs.

Facilitator: Which ones?

Attendee: The wooden ones in the media commons.

Facilitator: Great; what makes you choose those chairs over the ones near the café?

Attendee: Well, I go to the library for two hours between my Monday/Wednesday/Friday classes, and I find that the chairs in that area, while not as comfortable as the ones in the café, are located where I can get a better WiFi signal. They are also farther from the toilets, so that area is less distracting.

By asking *why* the person answered as he or she did, the library learned:

- that the responder uses the library as a landing spot between classes;
- that the library should consider other ways to make time between classes more comfortable and valuable for others who do the same;
- which chairs the responder feels are more comfortable;
- that the WiFi signal near the café may need to be stronger; and
- that the Road Map should address an acoustical problem related to the walls surrounding the toilets so users will be less distracted by unwanted noise.

Notes should be taken during the conversation to preserve comments and communicate to those participating that the library and consultant take what they have to say seriously. Figure 3.6 is an example of boards on easels used to capture comments from the public during an engagement meeting to discuss their aspirations for a new branch library.

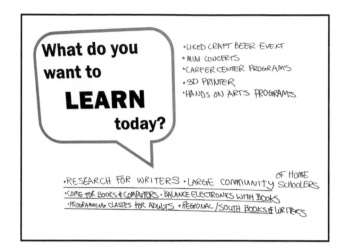

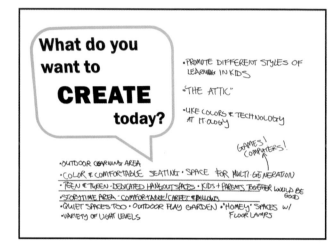

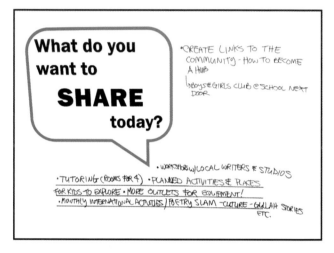

Figure 3.6. These are actual boards with notes taken in a community engagement meeting where members of the community discussed their aspirations for an upcoming library renovation.

Wrap-Up

Following the community conversation, it is important to bring the meeting officially to a close in a timely manner. Be sensitive and do not cut anyone off or adjourn so early that people are frustrated they did not get to speak; however, the meeting should end on time out of respect for everyone's schedules. If there are still some who feel the need to express their ideas or opinions, they should be invited to talk afterward. This is also important for those who are not comfortable speaking in front of a larger crowd.

In closing, the consultant or library representative should thank everyone for attending and participating, and briefly summarize the next steps in the process. Let those attending know when they should expect to hear more about the project and what the next steps are in the process. If there is a participatory exercise following the official closing of the meeting, it should be explained.

Participatory Exercise

Following the wrap-up, it is often helpful to have everyone participate in a short exit exercise in which they weigh in on what was said during the meeting by voting on what they feel were the important issues discussed or what they feel the three highest priorities should be; alternatively, they might be given the opportunity provide written comments regarding their favorite activities within the library and so on.

This exercise can take many different forms and can be as simple as handing out sticky notes and

 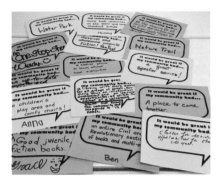 

Figure 3.7. Community members leave their final thoughts on an "exit ticket." This is an effective way to capture final thoughts and ideas that may not have been discussed during the meeting.

asking participants to write what they feel is the most important issue discussed. Another exercise offers attendees three different colored stickers representing their first, second, and third choices, and invites them to place their stickers next to the written notes from the meeting concerning the issues they feel are most important. Another effective exercise is to have attendees fill out exit tickets summarizing their most important takeaway from the meeting (see figure 3.7).

Whatever form the exercise takes, this can be an effective way to capture final thoughts, prioritize comments collected throughout the conversation, and promote impromptu, casual conversation among participants, the library representative, and the consultant.

02 ENGAGE | *listen*

DELIVERABLES

- Minutes from engagement process conversations

- Photographs and other documentation of engagement meetings

- Summary documentation of project issues, aspirations, and requests

- Survey results, if any

Figure 3.8. 02 Engage/Listen

STEP 3: PROGRAM/DEFINE

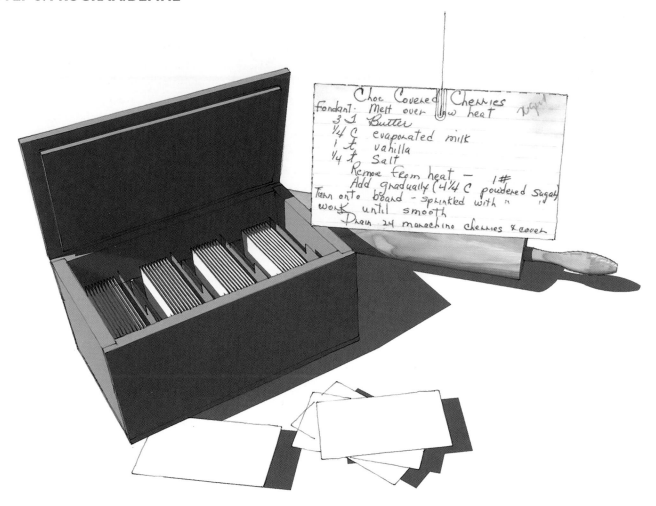

Figure 3.9. Recipe

Valuable information gained in steps 1 and 2 will help form goals to be achieved in the Road Map. However, for it to be useful, this information must be organized in a way that it is easily understood and quantifiable. The tool architects and planners use to document and organize this information is known as a *building program.*

What Is a Building Program?

Unlike programs hosted by library staff for the benefit of users, the term *program* in the context of Road Map planning means something entirely different. A building program is essentially the recipe for the library. Just as a recipe lists what ingredients to use, how much of each ingredient to measure, and the order in which each is to be mixed, the building program enumerates

what, how much, and in what order the components within a library are to be arranged. Building programs, like recipes, come in different shapes and sizes, but in all cases they contain these three descriptors.

In addition to the *quantifiable* information that answers the questions of what, how much, and in what order, more thorough building programs contain *qualitative* information such as required light levels, acoustical requirements, types of finishes, required technologies, equipment, and so on.

Usually this more-detailed information is not necessary for the development of a Road Map, but it should always be included prior to the commencement of the final design of a library facility. Put simply, a building program is the enumeration of the library's components and their spatial and environmental requirements.

The Purpose and Creation of a Building Program

Building programs describe the types of spaces needed in a facility to enable the desired activities within it to take place. Library building programs used to originate through standard formulas based on population projections, FTE calculations, square-foot-per-capita ratios, and so on. There was a plug-and-play aspect to their creation; for example, one would enter the projected population or FTEs for a specific community, and the formula would dictate the number of shelves and seats required. However, as libraries have evolved from being material-centric to people-centric, greater focus is placed on the activities and services the library should provide and less on what any particular ratio or rule of thumb might dictate. This is not to say that details such as collections, tables, and chairs are not important; it is just that when a building program is created for a Road Map, the tail should not wag the dog.

In developing library programs, careful consideration should be given to the user experience by thinking through the entire sequence of the user's visit to the library, beginning even before he or she enters the building. Borrowing from best practices in retail and service industries, libraries are seeking ways to transform the experiences of their users in meaningful ways. By trying to walk a mile in the user's shoes, common problems can be identified, service paradigms can be challenged, and unique design considerations can be developed—all to benefit the user. This is a much different way to formulate a building program than just plugging numbers into formulas (see figure 3.10).

The development of the building program evolves from a multitude of conversations and extended dialogue with those involved in the engagement process. Ideas are collected, quantified, and summarized in program drafts for the library's review and input. Revised drafts are produced, and the cycle is repeated until the building program clearly includes all the elements necessary to accomplish the library's vision. The development of a building program often benefits greatly from the close examination of professional lessons learned, approaches from other services industries, and a thorough evaluation of related case studies. The process of visiting other projects, whether in person or through published materials, allows planners to gain fresh ideas and insights, learn from others' successes and mistakes, and sometimes be inspired by others' creative solutions. This process is known as *benchmarking*. The time and expense invested in benchmarking is worth every penny (see figure 3.11).

LIBRARIES AND USER EXPERIENCE DESIGN

When I recall the built spaces of libraries as I learned them, images of rolling carts laden with books to be shelved, fingers strumming their way through card catalogs, and silent aisles of stacks come immediately to mind. However, when patrons articulate their needs related to libraries, they describe Internet connections, engaging programming, and materials of both digital and physical varieties available on demand. The built spaces of libraries are faced with the need for innovation to create a new sort of "library experience" for patrons. In a 2016 article for the *Journal of Library Innovation*, Valerie Graham and I suggested that user experience design (UXD) is a pathway to uncovering possibilities for the future of built space in libraries.

As libraries work to keep pace with the rapid influx of communication technologies, the built space of the library has reached an inflection point. Libraries are faced with the task of deciding how to allocate square footage for more programs and more access to technology while maintaining holdings and investing in digital infrastructure. And each library is different, with a specific mission and user population that, in tandem, drive its operations.

The notion of UXD for libraries revolves around human experience–both individual and collective–that occurs in the built and digital spaces of the library. In an article for the *American Clearinghouse on Educational Facilities Journal*, I offered that our human experience is formed in our relationships to the built spaces we inhabit. The built space offers us opportunities to mix formal and informal learning spaces for a variety of experiences. For libraries, this means engaging our users based on their needs and involving them in the design process.

As libraries begin to develop new service approaches, the spaces of libraries should be increasingly mission driven and user focused. The suburban library that serves families through programs might look (and be built) very different from the urban library serving as a career development center or community hub. The interiors of these libraries must flex to offer the resources and venues central to the mission, rather than necessarily maintaining the quiet, ordered storehouse model.

For most libraries, this user-centered approach begins with a look at two questions: "What is our mission?" and "What do our users need?" These two ideas function in concert, and both should be answered by a team of library staff members and users.

Then, based on the answers to these questions, libraries would do well to establish a Road Map that includes facility design, central practices, and resource needs. This process can and should involve the talents of not only the internal staff and users but also a team of architects, planners, and other mission-specific consultants or mentors who can drive the process forward.

For libraries, opportunities to focus on mission and consider how well-built space reflects that mission often turns the conversation directly to users and the user experience. This shift in focus from a materials-centered library to a user-centered library requires a reexamination of the built space of libraries.

–John S. McArthur

Associate Professor, Knight School of Communication
Queens University of Charlotte

Figure 3.10. Libraries and user experience design

BENCHMARKING

Benchmarking is the process of investigating other libraries and case studies for the purpose of examining best practices, creative solutions, and inventive approaches to inform the programming process. Learning from others and witnessing firsthand alternative approaches to common library challenges can be invaluable. It can be the most effective way to convince those trapped by current paradigms that other alternatives can be, and often are, better.

If traveling and visiting other libraries is not practical or affordable, reviewing case studies through documented visits by others or studying a compilation of published materials can also be an effective way to glean insight and learn lessons from others.

Benchmarking is most effective when it is done at the beginning of the programming process so that the enumerated list of spaces and elements can take into consideration new ideas and approaches that are born out of the benchmarking visits or the conversations that follow. Often the most effective ideas are derived from reacting to the failed attempts of others, so it is important to remember that it is just as important to study the failures of others as well as their successes. Furniture and product manufacturers often host benchmarking trips to introduce new and innovative approaches to consider. The image below was taken during a furniture manufacturer sponsored trip to benchmark several new libraries and to tour their furniture design facility to view new and innovative furniture products.

Figure 3.11. Benchmarking

Print Collections

While print collections alone may no longer be the yardstick for a library's effectiveness, importance, or stature, in many cases they are still a significant occupier of space within the library. When developing the building program for a Road Map, it is critical to carefully consider the future of the print collections within the library to determine if they are growing, leveling off, or shrinking. Recognizing that the answer will vary depending on the specific collection in question, each collection should be assessed and summarized in a Collection Summary that addresses the following issues.

Issue: What to Retain?

In determining what to retain, many factors must be considered in public and academic libraries alike, starting with the accessibility to the information digitally, in perpetuity, with full text and pictures. Other questions to be considered include: Should duplicates be kept, or not? What resources are accessible through partner libraries, institutions, and consumers? What materials will the public or faculty demand be available? When is the last time the collection has been weeded or managed? What are the circulation rates of the materials over the last five, ten, or twenty years?

Issue: Which Collections Will Grow or Diminish over Time?

Special collections and archives notwithstanding, it is important to ask which collections within the library will grow or diminish. Often the demographics of a community change, requiring the public library to expand collections and/or provide new resources. In academic settings, departments and degrees are added and dropped, and new pedagogies are developed. These changes result in new areas of emphasis within the collection. It is important not to assume every print collection will shrink or remain at current levels. The building program should account for this.

Issue: Where Should Retained Materials Be Located?

Once the size and contents of the collections have been determined, it is important to discuss where they will be located. In many cases the collections should remain in the existing library. However, in academic libraries this conversation should consider the advantages and disadvantages of off-site repositories. Questions regarding what is the best and highest use of the limited library square footage should be addressed. Off-site repositories can free up valuable space in a main library and allow for a less expensive way to store rarely accessed materials that are too valuable to discard. However, repositories require space, staff, and a plan for moving materials to and from their location when needed. See chapter 4 for a more detailed analysis of high-density storage options that impact the size and cost of an off-site repository solution.

Issue: How Should What Remains Be Stored or Displayed?

Traditionally, most large print collections are housed in tall, 90-inch-high double-faced (DF) shelving units organized in rows (ranges). These DF units vary in width from 18-to-24-inch wide (and wider in special cases). If for no reason other than cost, it often makes sense to reuse this shelving when possible, making any adjustments necessary to accommodate ADA requirements for aisle width.

In some cases, however, taller shelving may be replaced with lower shelving on casters for greater mobility and flexibility within the library. Other times, materials are reshelved into more efficient shelving systems that reduce the physical footprint of the collections. The collection summary should specify the desired type, height, and configuration of the shelving to be used for each collection, including the number of shelves per side that will actually hold materials. (For example, many public libraries prefer not to shelve material on the top or bottom shelves.) As decisions regarding how the collections will be shelved are made, the collection summary will translate the number of required shelves into the required area (square footage) needed.

Collection Summary

It is important to acknowledge how differently architects and librarians think about print collections. Generally, librarians think about these collections in terms of volumes, items, or titles, while architects and planners need to convert these quantities into square feet and the area they occupy. A collection summary does this, and also provides an overview of how the print collections should be shelved.

Figure 3.12 is an excerpt of a collection summary from a both a small public branch and an academic library.

COLLECTION	COLLECTION BY VOLUMES								SHELVING CONFIGURATION			AREA
A	B	C	D	E	F	G	H	I	O	P	Q	R
	TOTAL COLLECTION (IN VOLUMES)	PROJECTED REDUCTION	PROJECTED INCREASE	% OF COLLECTION ON SHELVES	VOLUMES TO BE SHELVED	VOLUMES PER LF	ADJUSTMENT FACTOR	TOTAL LF REQUIRED	# OF SHELVES PER SIDE	# OF DF UNITS	SF PER DF UNIT	TOTAL SF
CIRCULATING COLLECTION												
A&B *Gen, Phil, Psy, Rel*	3,025	0%	0%	100%	3,025	8	1.5	567	5	19	20	380
C,D,E,F,G *Hist, Fla, Anthro, Sports*	6,900	0%	0%	100%	6,900	8	1.5	1,294	3	72	20	1,440
HA–HJ *Business*	3,000	0%	0%	100%	3,000	8	1.5	563	5	19	20	380
HC, J, K, L *Soc Sci, Pol Sci, Law, Ed*	5,700	0%	0%	100%	5,700	8	1.5	1,069	5	36	20	720
M *Music*	900	0%	0%	100%	900	8	1.5	169	5	6	20	120
N *Art*	3,000	0%	0%	100%	3,000	8	1.5	563	5	19	20	380
P *Literature*	20,000	0%	0%	100%	20,000	8	1.5	3,750	5	125	20	2,500
Q *Science*	3,000	0%	0%	100%	3,000	8	1.5	563	5	19	20	380
R *Medicine*	3,000	0%	0%	100%	3,000	8	1.5	563	5	19	20	380
S–Z *Tech, Military, Library Sci*	2,375	0%	0%	100%	2,375	8	1.5	445	5	15	20	380
JUVENILE PRINT												
New Books	275	0%	0%	70%	193	6	1.5	48	3	3	20	60
Juv Picture Books	5,540	0%	20%	80%	5,318	20	1.5	399	3	23	20	460
Juv Fiction	3,860	0%	20%	80%	3,706	15	1.5	371	5	13	20	260
Juv Non Fic	1,500	0%	0%	90%	1,350	15	1.5	135	5	5	20	100
Board Books	700	0%	0%	100%	700	6	1.5	175	5	6	20	120
ADULT PRINT												
New Books	300	0%	0%	70%	210	6	1.5	53	5	2	20	40
Fiction	7,400	0%	20%	70%	6,216	8	1.5	1,166	3	39	20	780
Non Fiction	5000	0%	5%	80%	4,200	7	1.5	900	5	30	20	600
Large Print	800	0%	0%	85%	680	7	1.5	146	5	5	20	100
Oversized	240	0%	0%	95%	228	6	1.5	57	5	3	20	60

Figure 3.12. Collection summary—volumes

Sizing the Collections

- In the collection summary shown in figure 3.12, columns A and B list the different print collections and corresponding total volume counts for each that will remain in the existing facility. (If the print collections will be housed in multiple locations, such as a repository, for example, an individual collection summary should be provided for each separate physical collection.) These collection descriptions and volume counts are provided by the library staff.

- Columns C and D denote any projected reductions or increases to each collection that should be taken into account.

- Column E lists the percentage of each collection that will be shelved in the library at any given time by taking into account the average circulation rate for each. This is particularly important for public libraries, where there is always some portion of the collections in circulation. In academic libraries, however, it is recommended that this always be 100 percent, since most items are returned at certain points during the year, and because as circulation rates for print materials decline, more will remain on the shelves.

- Column F factors columns B, C, D, and E together to arrive at the total volumes in each collection that need to be shelved.

- Column G lists the average number of volumes per linear foot for each collection. This recognizes that items in different collections vary in widths, and therefore the number of items that can fit on one linear foot of shelving will vary. There are many different standards published and used by

consultants; however, this number can be verified by sampling the collection in question and counting the number of items in a 12-inch space.

- Column H is a multiplier that factors the total linear feet (LF) required for each collection to determine the amount of each shelf that should remain empty. For instance, if the library would like 12 inches (one-third) of a standard 36-inch shelf to be empty, then 24 inches (two-thirds) of the shelf will be occupied by materials. Therefore:

$$(24" \text{ of materials}) \times (\text{a factor of } 1.5) = 36" \text{ of required shelving}$$

Obviously, this factor changes depending on the amount of empty space the library prefers to have on each shelf and can vary among the different collections.

- Column I calculates the entries in columns F, G, and H to arrive at the total LF necessary to shelve the collection.

In some cases it is easier to calculate the LF a collection currently occupies by measuring its footprint on each shelf rather than beginning with the volume count and circulation rate produced from the library's catalog software. Assuming this number reflects the typical number of items not in circulation at any given time, the total LF of that collection only needs to be adjusted for any projected increases or decreases and the amount of empty space desired for each shelf to arrive at the total LF necessary to shelve the collection. Figure 3.13 depicts a collection summary that outlines this approach.

COLLECTION	COLLECTION BY OCCUPIED LF OF SHELVING				
A	**J**	**K**	**L**	**M**	**N**
	LF CURRENTLY OCCUPIED	PROJECTED INCREASE	LF CURRENTLY OCCUPIED	ADJUSTMENT FACTOR	TOTAL LF REQUIRED
CIRCULATING COLLECTION					
A&B *Gen, Phil, Psy, Rel*	378	0%	0%	1.5	567
C,D,E,F,G *Hist, Fla, Anthro, Sports*	863	0%	0%	1.5	1,294
HA–HJ *Business*	375	0%	0%	1.5	563
HC, J, K, L *Soc Sci, Pol Sci, Law, Ed*	713	0%	0%	1.5	1,069
M *Music*	113	0%	0%	1.5	169
N *Art*	375	0%	0%	1.5	563
P *Literature*	2,500	0%	0%	1.5	3,750
Q *Science*	375	0%	0%	1.5	563
R *Medicine*	375	0%	0%	1.5	563
S–Z *Tech, Military, Library Sci*	297	0%	0%	1.5	445
JUVENILE PRINT					
New Books	32	0%	0%	1.5	48
Juv Picture Books	222	0%	20%	1.5	399
Juv Fiction	206	0%	20%	1.5	371
Juv Non Fic	90	0%	0%	1.5	135
Board Books	117	0%	0%	1.5	175
ADULT PRINT					
New Books	35	0%	0%	1.5	53
Fiction	648	0%	20%	1.5	1,166
Non Fiction	571	0%	5%	1.5	900
Large Print	97	0%	0%	1.5	146
Oversized	38	0%	0%	1.5	57

Figure 3.13. Collection summary—linear feet

Shelving the Collections

Once the total LF necessary to shelve the collection is determined, the next question to answer is: How will it be shelved? (Refer again to figure 3.12.)

- Column O identifies the number of shelves on each side of a DF shelving unit that will hold materials. For example, many public libraries that have 90-inch high traditional metal shelving with seven shelves per side prefer to keep the top and bottom shelves empty; therefore, only five shelves per side will hold materials
- Column P denotes the number of DF units required to contain the collection by dividing Column I by the available LF of each DF unit as determined by the number of shelves per side specified in Column O; that is:

> Total LF necessary to shelve the collection
> ÷ Total LF of each DF unit that will hold materials
> _____
> = Total # of DF units required

The number of LF per DF unit is calculated by multiplying the desired number of shelves per side to be used by the number of sides per DF unit (which is two) by the length of each shelf (which is 3 feet). So if the library wants a particular collection to occupy only five shelves per side of a DF unit, Column I is divided by 30. In other words:

$$(5 \text{ shelves per side}) \times (2 \text{ sides per DF unit}) \times (3' \text{ per shelf}) = 30LF \text{ per DF unit}$$

- Column Q assigns the amount of SF that each DF unit will occupy in the library. This number takes into account the width of the DF units selected and desired aisle width between the ranges.
- Column R calculates the total area in the library needed to house the collection.

At first glance, these calculations might seem tedious; however, it is critical to think intentionally about the space that print collections will occupy in the library moving forward. Remember, if the goal of the Road Map is to utilize every square foot of space in the library for its best and highest use, then the area dedicated to the print collections should be only what is essential to serve the library's community.

The collection summary is an important tool that adds to the information gathered in steps 1 and 2 to inform the overall building program. With the programmatic goals clearly defined, the next step is to develop the conceptual design that will become the basis for the vision outlined in the Road Map.

03 PROGRAM | *define*

DELIVERABLES

- Collection summary
- Building program summary document

Figure 3.14. 03 Program/Define

STEP 4: DESIGN/PLAN

At this point in the Road Map process, the starting point is documented through the information gathered in step 1 and graphically represented in the existing floor and furniture plans. Through the work in steps 2 and 3, the programmatic goals for the reenvisioned library are established in the building program. The effort and decisions made to this point form the basis for the work in step 4 to begin. This is where the written words take shape graphically through the iterative conceptual design process.

Conceptual Design Process

When developing a Road Map for an existing library, the conceptual design process examines possibilities and options for how the programmatic elements can be organized and arranged within the existing facility. Metaphorically speaking, the roof of the existing library is removed and the building turned upside down, emptying all of its contents. The conceptual design process then searches for the most creative, practical, and efficient way to put the new programmatic elements back in. If all the newly defined programmatic elements will

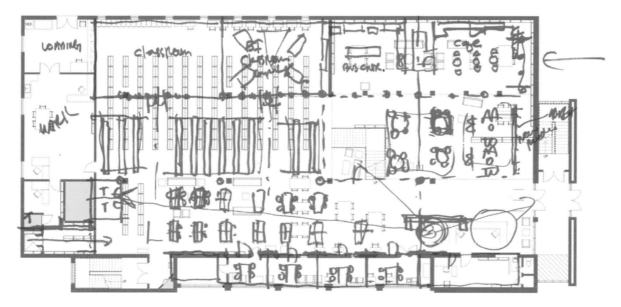

EXISTING FIRST FLOOR PLAN

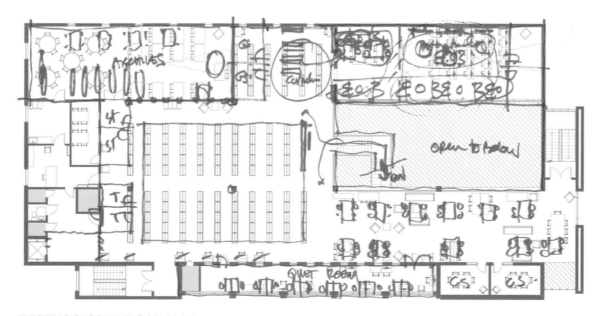

EXISTING SECOND FLOOR PLAN

Figure 3.15. Conceptual sketches developed during the Road Map design step

not fit into the existing building, then alternative strategies are investigated, including possible additions to the existing library.

The goal of the conceptual design process is to offer a fresh perspective and see beyond the paradigms established through years of living in a space and assuming certain conditions and configurations are written in stone. Working in a library for years in less-than-ideal circumstances often blinds staff to possibilities that are relatively easy to achieve. The familiar "boiling a frog" parable describes a situation in which gradual change over a long period of time can lead to undesirable consequences before one even realizes it is happening. Similarly, a library can grow obsolete, inefficient, and ineffective through years of subtle change without anyone realizing it.

The end result of this step in the Road Map process is to arrive at a conceptual design that addresses as many of the library's programmatic goals as possible. Remember, the plan that achieves the most goals for the most people is the most successful.

Figure 3.15 shows sketches developed during the conceptual design process for a small academic library Road Map highlighted as one of the case studies in chapter 7. The green lines represent spaces and furniture layered over the existing floor plans to study how the new programmatic elements identified in the building program

might fit into the existing structure. Many alternative options were evaluated at this step in the process to determine the optimal conceptual design.

Conceptual Design versus Final Design

It is important to distinguish that the conceptual design developed for the Road Map is not a detailed or final design that has every issue completely resolved. The conceptual design examines the library from a high-altitude, global perspective. The spaces, rooms, and furniture are merely placeholders; the specifics will be defined later when an architect and interior designer are hired to develop the final design for that portion of the Road Map. Until then, the conceptual design focuses more on getting spaces sized appropriately, verifying the correct quantities of library components, and establishing ideal adjacencies and locations for the internal library functions.

It is important to note that the architect or consultant hired to develop the Road Map does not necessarily have to be the same person hired to produce the final design. The hiring of a consultant for the Road Map and the final design of the library space often involve two different procurement procedures and contracts. These can be, but do not have to be, done by the same person or firm.

An Iterative Process

Figure 3.16. Design review taking place during an all-day on-site charrette to solicit everyone's ideas on the concepts being considered

An *iterative process* is one where the desired result is achieved through the means of a repeated cycle of operations in which each iteration leads to a better outcome. This is the design process. The consultant will use the building program from step 3 and the existing floor and furniture plans from step 1 to produce initial conceptual floor plans for the library's review and input. Through the dialogue that ensues, the consultant will revise the plans to more closely respond to the library's comments and vision. This process repeats until the library and architect feel that the conceptual design best represents the Road Map's ideal final destination.

The collaborative iterative process often involves what is known as a *charrette*. Charrettes can be organized as single- or multi-day events where the consultant and design team camp out on-site and involve the library or users in an intense design workshop to study and vet a multitude of ideas, seeking immediate input and feedback that expedites the process. This collaboration saves time and allows suggested ideas and what-if scenarios to be studied in real time.

04 DESIGN | *plan*

DELIVERABLES

- Proposed floor plans and other diagrams

- Summary of measurable benefits of the conceptual design compared to current conditions

Figure 3.17. 04 Design/Plan

RENDERINGS

A LARGE RESEARCH UNIVERSITY LIBRARY

One of the by-products of the conceptual design process is the ability to quickly create three-dimensional imagery that can be used to communicate the future vision, create excitement, and help in fund-raising efforts. The renderings shown below were developed for a large research university library to illustrate to potential donors what the completed research commons space might look like.

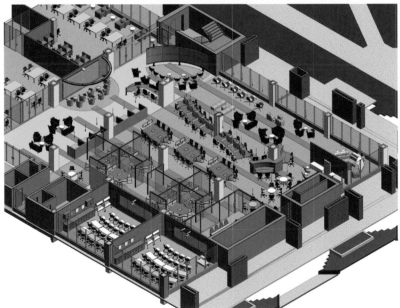

Three-Dimensional Axonometric Floor Plan

Figure 3.18. Renderings

STEP 5: PHASING/STRATEGIZE

The Road Map approach has been essential in creating successful and expedient change. The phasing aspect allows certain changes to be made independent of the availability of funding for the entire project. So progress is possible incrementally, and this actionable aspect of the Road Map is morale boosting. When it comes to progress, doing trumps not doing, but having an accepted, well-thought-out plan "lubricates" positive, successful change. (Dana Sally, Dean of Libraries [Retired], Western Carolina University)

Guiding Principles for Phasing Plans

- The goal is for each area, group, or department in the library to have to move only once and never more than twice. In the event that an area, group, or department's first move is to a temporary location or swing space, its second move should be into the final location.
- Each phase should be able to stand on its own. If the implementation occurs over a long period of time or through separate funding mechanisms, each phase should be able to stand on its own and not leave the impression that the library is operating in an unfinished renovation. Ideally, each phase or group of phases can take place as a small, independent renovation.
- The phases should correspond to mechanical units, systems, or zones to the extent possible so that infrastructure and above-ceiling work can be addressed simultaneously with the physical alterations. The goal is to eliminate having to go back and work further in an area that has been completed in a prior phase.
- Phases are often subdivided into multiple steps or subphases. These can also be executed independently if funds are limited.
- During each phase, access to the building entrances, service points, toilet facilities, elevators (if any), and emergency exits must be maintained. Thought should also be given to how and where the contractor will access and stage the work in each phase.
- Collections, shelving, and furniture moves and storage should also be planned for in the phasing plan. This often involves creating staging space within the library that serves as temporary storage for items in between phases.

Figure 3.19 illustrates the concepts behind developing a phasing plan for the execution of a Road Map. It is similar to old-fashioned slide puzzles, except for the fact that any tile can jump to the open space. The arrangement of the numbers 1–5 on tile 1 represents the existing conditions in the library. The final vision of the Road Map is to have the numbers in the correct order using minimal steps, with as many numbers as possible only moving once.

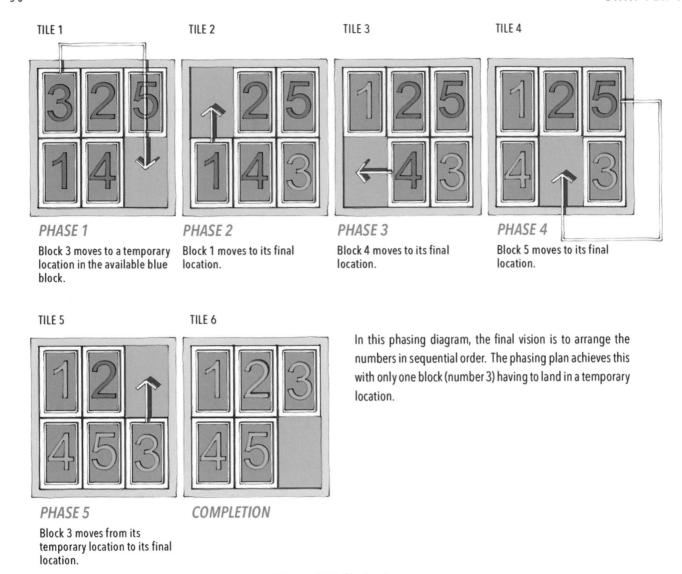

In this phasing diagram, the final vision is to arrange the numbers in sequential order. The phasing plan achieves this with only one block (number 3) having to land in a temporary location.

Figure 3.19. Phasing diagram

Following the creation of the phased implementation plan, cost estimates should be developed for the entire Road Map or for individual phases to be executed as standalone projects. Examples of finished phasing plans are shown in the case studies in chapter 7.

05   PHASING | *strategize*

DELIVERABLE

- Phasing plans

Figure 3.20. 05 Phasing/Strategize

STEP 6: ESTIMATE/BUDGET

At this point in the Road Map process, the typical response is, "This is great! But what will it cost?" or "What will it cost to do phases 1, 2, and 3?" This is always the question, and in a traditional master plan, it is an all-or-nothing proposition with a large price tag.

The Road Map approach however, enables the library or owner[1] to move one step or phase at a time by funding individual steps and phases as resources allow and opportunities present themselves. It offers flexibility for immediate smaller renovations, rather than waiting for long periods of time for all the funding to be identified while, in the meantime, nothing happens to the physical space. Whether estimating the entire Road Map or just a single phase of it, the estimate should reflect all the expenses related to the work. This is known as the *total project cost*.

Total Project Cost

The total project cost for any project—whether a new building, an entire renovation, or a single phase of a Road Map—comprises hard costs (the construction cost) and soft costs (everything not included in the construction cost). It is helpful to think of the total project cost as the entire pie and the hard and soft costs as slices (see figure 3.21). For a more detailed explanation of the total project cost, see chapter 5.

To answer the question "How much will the Road Map—or a particular phase of it—cost?" the consultant develops an estimate for the scope of work in question. This estimate is general in nature, as it is based on conceptual drawings instead of the fully detailed drawings and specifications typical for a final design. However, the estimate needs to be reliable for planning purposes. In order to do this the consultant authoring the Road Map begins with estimating the Road Map's hard costs.

Hard Costs

The hard costs associated with a project are comprised of the construction and site-related costs paid to the contractor and his or her subcontractors for their services. For the purposes of the Road Map, we will consider the term *hard costs* synonymous with *construction cost*. The only owner expense typically included in this number involves construction services that contribute to the transformation of the physical space that are performed by the owner. For example, if a contractor is hired to renovate a phase in the Road Map but the owner wants to handle the painting, then the owner's costs associated with that work should be added to the construction cost.

To estimate the construction cost, the consultant either develops it on his or her own or engages a professional cost estimator who knows the local market conditions and understands how to develop a cost estimate

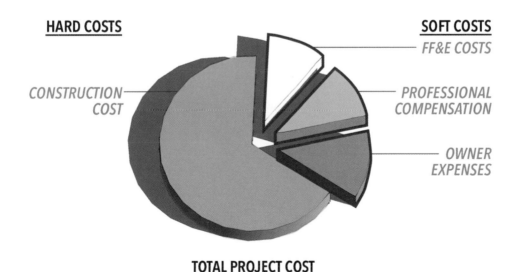

HARD COSTS   **SOFT COSTS**

FF&E COSTS

CONSTRUCTION COST

PROFESSIONAL COMPENSATION

OWNER EXPENSES

TOTAL PROJECT COST

Figure 3.21. Pie chart

1. For the purposes of this book it may be helpful to think of the term *owner* as synonymous with *library*; however, with regard to financial, budget, and contractual considerations, the term *owner* may more appropriately refer to the funding or contracting agency that works on behalf of or represents the library, such as a county or university facilities department.

from conceptual design documents that provide very little detail. Because of the inherent lack of detail in the conceptual design documents, the consultant often develops written and diagrammatic narratives for various phases of the Road Map that are to be estimated to help define the scope of work envisioned. Figure 3.22 is an example of a diagram informing the estimator of the anticipated work to be included.

PLAN NOTES

1. Wall in this location to be interior painted hollow metal framing to match existing adjacent interior hollow metal frames.

2. New millwork work surface, typical.

3. Low wall built to receive 42"-high library shelving and sectional furniture.

4. Demolish porcelain paver tiles and prep slab for new carpet tiles. Existing lighting to be removed and replaced with new Elliptipar wall sconces in lobby.

5. New millwork circulation desk with quartz countertops.

6. Study rooms to receive new built-in millwork work surfaces. All doors on study rooms to be full glass for maximum visibility.

7. New 2x2 ceiling grid with new 2x4 lighting configuration to be installed in highlighted area.

8. New linear direct / indirect light fixtures over stack area.

9. Assume all new finishes including carpet, paint, and ceiling tiles. New lay-in light fixtures as well, UNO.

10. All individual study rooms to have built-in millwork counters. All doors to be full glass.

11. Built-in booths with new upholstered cushions.

12. Install floor boxes for power and data in existing slab for computer area, one per table.

13. All spaces to receive new carpet and base, and new paint on walls and soffits, UNO. All new walls to be 3 5/8" metal stud with 1 layer of 5/8" gypsum board on each side, UNO. New carpet to be carpet tiles. The rooms shaded in gray do not receive any new finishes.

Figure 3.22. The more information that can be provided to the estimator explaining the scope of work and the level of finishes to be included in that phase, the more accurate the estimate will be.

Based on the Road Map's conceptual design and the diagrammatic narrative depicted in figure 3.22, a professional estimator was engaged to develop estimates for all four phases of a Road Map for a small, single-story public library that totaled 22,458 SF. Figure 3.23 is an excerpt from that estimate summarizing the estimated costs for all four phases of the work and includes a breakdown of the costs for phase 1. The estimator's deliverable provided detailed breakdowns for the other phases as well, but these are not included here.

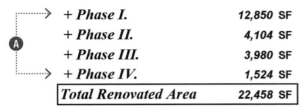

Renovated Areas:

+ Phase I.	12,850	SF
+ Phase II.	4,104	SF
+ Phase III.	3,980	SF
+ Phase IV.	1,524	SF
Total Renovated Area	**22,458**	**SF**

Project Cost Summary:

	TOTAL COST	COST/SF	% OF COST
+ Phase I.	$340,711	$26.51	62.88%
+ Phase II.	$121,393	$29.58	22.40%
+ Phase III.	$65,765	$16.52	12.14%
+ Phase IV.	$13,951	$9.15	2.57%
Total Estimated Construction Cost	$541,820	$24.13	100.00%

PHASE I. Probable Construction Cost Summary		TOTAL COST	COST/SF	% OF COST
02 SITE WORK		$0	$0.00	0.00%
02 SELECTIVE DEMOLITION		$11,786	$0.92	3.46%
03 CONCRETE		$6,466	$0.50	1.90%
06 WOOD & PLASTICS		$32,452	$2.53	9.52%
07 MOISTURE & THERMAL PROTECTION		$2,505	$0.19	0.74%
08 DOORS AND WINDOWS		$39,805	$3.10	11.68%
09 FINISHES		$120,370	$9.37	35.33%
10 SPECIALTIES		$750	$0.06	0.22%
11 EQUIPMENT		$0	$0.00	0.00%
12 FURNISHINGS		$0	$0.00	0.00%
15 PLUMBING		$0	$0.00	0.00%
15 FIRE PROTECTION		$3,400	$0.26	1.00%
15 HVAC		$3,783	$0.29	1.11%
16 ELECTRICAL SYSTEMS		$19,455	$1.51	5.71%
SUBTOTAL		$240,772	$18.74	70.67%
MARK-UPS				
- Sales Tax		$1,729	$0.13	0.51%
- Labor Burden		$1,553	$0.12	0.46%
- General Requirements		$9,762	$0.76	2.87%
- Overhead		$7,614	$0.59	2.23%
- Profit		$18,300	$1.42	5.37%
- Bonding & Insurance		$4,196	$0.33	1.23%
SUBTOTAL		$283,926	$22.10	83.33%
*Design Contingency	15.00%	$42,589	$3.31	12.50%
*Escalation Contingency	5.00%	$14,196	$1.10	4.17%
Total Estimated Probable Construction Cost: *Phase I.*		$340,711	$26.51	100.00%

Figure 3.23. Detailed estimate

- The *Project Area* shows the building area included in each phase in the Road Map.
- The *Probable Construction Cost Summary* enumerates the estimator's breakdown of his estimate by the standard sixteen specification divisions used by contractors. This indicates how the overall cost is divided among various project categories, such as demolition, doors, walls, ceilings, plumbing, lighting, HVAC, and so on. In this example, the furnishings number in line 12 is $0 because the furniture is not included in the contractor's scope of work; in this case, it is a soft-cost item that will be provided by the owner.
- *Mark-Ups* are fees and expenses incurred by the contractor, amounting to almost 15 percent of the subtotal.
- *Contingencies* are normally included in estimates for conceptual designs because of the number of assumptions the estimator must make due to the unknowns inherent with a Road Map.

  The Design Contingency accounts for the lack of detail, allowing for design features or materials that might be included in the final design but are not specified in the Road Map's conceptual design documents.

  The Escalation Contingency is an allowance for increases in market conditions between the time the estimate is developed and the actual anticipated construction period.
- The *Total Estimated Probable Construction Cost: Phase I* amount of $277,365 is the total construction cost that must be added to the soft costs to arrive at the estimated total project cost estimate.

Soft Costs

As noted earlier, soft costs comprise everything that is not included in the construction cost. Generally these costs can be organized into three categories: FF&E,

professional compensation, and owner expenses. A detailed explanation of these categories can be found in chapter 5.

Again answering the question "How much will the Road Map—or a particular phase of it—cost?" the consultant must also develop estimates for the soft cost related to the work. These are added to the construction cost estimate to arrive at the total project cost estimate.

Determining the *FF&E costs* for the entire Road Map or an individual phase begins with an assessment of the existing furniture, shelving, and nontechnological equipment that is to be reused. Usually this is determined through a painstaking inventory process in which the consultant examines every piece of furniture within the library to determine what, if anything, can and should be reused. Once this is determined, those pieces are assigned a final location in the Road Map. In other words, just because a table designated for reuse is currently in a conference room does not necessarily mean it won't be better used elsewhere in the final design. Once final locations for all the reused pieces are determined, the amount of required new furniture in each phase can be determined and assigned a cost.

Figure 3.24 depicts an existing and proposed furniture plan for the small public library whose construction cost estimate was discussed earlier. The blue highlighted furniture on the existing plan indicates furniture designated for reuse during the furniture inventory assessment by the library and consultant. The proposed plan highlights in blue the locations of the reused furniture in the proposed design. On this drawing, furniture not highlighted in blue denotes new furniture that is needed and will be estimated in each phase accordingly.

Based on the proposed plan in figure 3.24, the consultant was able to provide detailed estimates for all refinishing and reupholstering of the existing furniture designated for reuse, along with detailed estimates for all the new pieces not highlighted in blue.

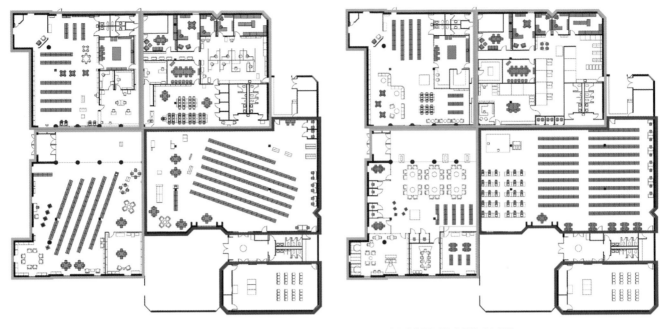

EXISTING FLOOR PLAN   PROPOSED FLOOR PLAN

Furniture highlighted in blue has been selected to be reused in the proposed plan.

- Phase 1A
- Phase 1B
- Phase 2
- Phase 3
- Phase 4

Figure 3.24. The areas outlined in various colors denote the extent of the Road Map's four phases, and correspond to the phases, described in figure 3.23.

Figure 3.25 is an excerpt from the furniture estimate summarizing the estimated furniture costs for each phase and itemizing the costs for the new items required for phase 1A of the Road Map.

The costs for equipment, including technology, whether for the entire Road Map or an individual phase, can vary from $0 to a substantial amount depending on the nature of the space within the library being addressed. In spaces where technology is the focus, such as information/learning/research commons, small-group collaborative spaces, and digital media studios, it is not uncommon for the consultant to engage a technology or A/V consultant to work with the library to define the scope of those and any other low-voltage systems that may need to be included in that particular phase. In more sophisticated library systems or academic institutions, there are often A/V and technology staff in house who are integral and play a key role in determining the scope and costs of the equipment and infrastructure that must be included in the total project cost estimate. In the case of the small public library, an equipment allowance was included in the Road Map estimate for each phase.

Professional compensation is another category listed as a soft cost. As the consultant is putting together the total project cost estimate, he or she should add a budget figure to cover these expenses. Some institutions, such as state agencies, have tables that provide allowable ranges for architectural and engineering design services. In the absence of any standards, the consultant should estimate those costs in light of comparable professional services fees in that particular geographic region.

Owner expenses vary, ranging from predesign activities, including Road Map exercises, to design and construction phase expenses to postconstruction expenses leading up to the ribbon cutting. Chapter 5 provides more detail on the various expenses that are included in this category.

FURNITURE ESTIMATE

PHASE 1A	$57,900.00
PHASE 1B	$116,735.00
PHASE 2	$23,565.00
PHASE 3	$32,795.00
PHASE 4	$3,200.00

PHASE 1A

	QTY.	ITEM DESCRIPTION	UNIT PRICE	EXTENDED PRICE
STACKS 32				
	1	90" ANCHOR DOWN INSTALL	$8,500.00	$8,500.00
	1	90" GUSSET INSTALL	$6,000.00	$6,000.00
	40	DF WOOD END PANEL, 90/20	$750.00	$30,000.00
	34	READING CHAIR, EXISTING (C1)	$0.00	$0.00
	6	READING TABLE, EXISTING (T1)	$0.00	$0.00
	10	INDIVIDUAL READING CARREL	$350.00	$3500.00
	*	(*existing shelving will be reused)	$0.00	$0.00
COMPUTERS 36				
	2	CHAIR, TASK STOOL AT PUBLIC SERVICE DESK	$600.00	$1,200.00
	26	CHAIR, COMPUTER, EXISTING (C5)	$0.00	$0.00
	4	CHAIR, COMPUTER, TO MATCH EXISTING	$300.00	$1,200.00
	30	COMPUTER TABLE	$250.00	$7,500.00
TOTAL PHASE 1A PRICING				**$57,900.00**

Figure 3.25. Furniture estimate

Summary

Figure 3.26 illustrates a total project cost estimate that totals all the hard and soft costs for all four phases of the Road Map for the small public library. This Road Map represents a fairly simple four-phase renovation, and the estimated construction and FF&E costs provided are several years old and certainly do not represent reliable cost-estimating numbers for use in current planning efforts. Estimated costs developed for each Road Map will vary greatly and are dependent on the project scope, current economic climate, and local market conditions. These are just a few of the variables that can affect the total project cost; however, this example does illustrate the basic components of a total project cost estimate and how it can be broken down into smaller sequential phases.

		PHASE 1 12,850 SF	PHASE 2 4,104 SF	PHASE 3 3,980 SF	PHASE 4 1,524 SF	LINE TOTALS
	HARD COSTS					
A	CONSTRUCTION COST ESTIMATE	$277,365.00	$112,513.00	$57,153.00	$8,632.00	**$455,663.00**
	SOFT COSTS					
	FF&E COSTS					
B.1	FF&E *Phase 1A* / *Phase 1B*	$57,900.00 / $116,735.00	$23,565.00	$32,795.00	$3,200.00	**$390,495.00**
B.2	FF&E ACCESSORIES	$8,732.00	$1,178.00	$1,640.00	$160.00	
B.3	TAXES AND SHIPPING	$18,337.00	$2,474.00	$3,443.00	$336.00	
B.4	TECHNOLOGY	$50,000.00	$30,000.00	$20,000.00	$20,000.00	
	PROFESSIONAL COMPENSATION					
C.1	ARCHITECTURAL/ENGINEERING BASIC SERVICES	$38,000.00	$8,000.00	$12,000.00	$2,000.00	**$81,000.00**
C.2	INTERIOR DESIGN FEE	$15,000.00	$2,000.00	$2,000.00	$2,000.00	
	OWNER EXPENSES					
D	OWNER PROJECT CONTINGENCY	$3,000.00	$30,000.00	$10,000.00	$2,000.00	**$72,000.00**

** *Note: Because design and escalation contingencies are included in the construction cost estimated on Line A, the owner project contingency allows for miscellaneous owner expenses, such as hazardous material surveys, construction testing, etc.*

TOTAL PROJECT COST ESTIMATE (BY PHASE):	$612,0169.00	$209,730.00	$139,031.00	$38,328.00	

TOTAL PROJECT COST ESTIMATE: $999,158.00

Figure 3.26. Total project cost estimate by phase

06   ESTIMATING | *budget*

DELIVERABLES

- Cost estimates for designated phases or the entire project included in the Road Map

- FF&E estimates based on new and reused items

- A comprehensive estimated total project budget, including all designated phases. See chapter 5 for more details.

Figure 3.27. 06 Estimate/Budget

4

COLLECTION STORAGE STRATEGIES

The elephants in the room are the various print collections within the existing library. Whether in a public or academic library, the question remains: "How has digital media affected the collections' use and growth, currently and over time?" The answer may involve some conjecture, depending on how far in the future one speculates, but recent Road Maps suggest that print collections, excluding special collections and archives, are being used and accessed less often. In fact, most academic libraries report a circulation rate in the mid-20-percent range for their general collections. One recent academic library wrestled with this issue when developing its Road Map.

Example: A midwestern university library's general collection occupied 6,000 DF shelving units. The question was asked: "Of the items the library has owned for more than ten years, what number has been checked out or used and reshelved during that time?" The library discovered that only about 25 percent of its collection was used during that time, which means approximately 4,500 DF shelving units of materials had most likely not been touched in more than a decade. That is the equivalent of approximately 90,000 SF of the building not used to its potential.

4,500 DF shelves × 20SF / DF Shelf = 90,000 SF

To build that much usable space in a new building with a 40 percent net-to-gross factor (see figure 4.1) would require a 126,000 SF building at a cost of at least $31 million and probably much more. That does not even include the soft costs associated with a building of that size, such as fees, technology and furniture, and so on.

126,000 SF × $250/SF = $31,500,000

It is not to say that all 4,500 DF shelves of material in the example above are not important and should be weeded or deaccessioned. In fact, there are a variety of reasons to keep materials that have not been touched in over a decade, but it is important to ask whether that is the best and most efficient use of 90,000 SF of space in a prominent building in a prime location. If not, then what are the options?

Assuming the collection has been reduced through weeding and deaccessioning to a point that the library or institution believes is appropriate and reasonable, the remaining items are usually stored through one or a combination of the following methods. The storage methods selected depend on any number of variables, including cost, space, structural capacity, size of the collection, accessibility, and so on. These methods include traditional shelving, compact shelving, high-bay storage, and automated storage and retrieval systems.

UNDERSTANDING SQUARE FEET

During the programming process and in the program documents, architects and the program documents will use the terms *net square feet* (NSF), *adjusted net square feet* (ANSF), and *gross square feet* (GSF). Below is an explanation for those terms and the difference between them.

In simple terms, net square feet represents the actual footprint an item occupies or the wall-to-wall space within a room. In image A, the footprint of a small reading table and its chairs totals 30 NSF.

The adjusted net square feet for that same table and chairs includes the surrounding usable floor area that, for all practical purposes, cannot be used for other functions. In image B, the illustrated 100 ANSF includes the immediate circulation space surrounding the table and chairs.

Gross square feet totals the ANSF of all the items within a space or facility and adds the square footage of all the supporting areas, such as general circulation space, mechanical rooms, toilets, wall thicknesses between the rooms, and so on, by multiplying the total ANSF by a net-to-gross multiplier.

For example, image C illustrates a small library addition with five group study rooms, each with an area of 100 ANSF. The gross square footage for that addition would equal the ANSF of those rooms plus all the area needed for supporting elements such as wall thicknesses, corridors, and mechanical space.

The total GSF of the addition in image C is 910 SF (32.5' x 28'). The difference between the total ANSF of the five group study rooms and the GSF of the addition represents the net-to-gross factor. (910 total GSF) – (500 total ANSF) = (a net-to-gross markup of 410 SF) or, in this case, a multiplier of approximately 1.9.

The 1.9 net-to-gross multiplier is unusually high because the example in image C is small. Typically for library buildings the net-to-gross multiplier ranges from 1.4 to 1.5.

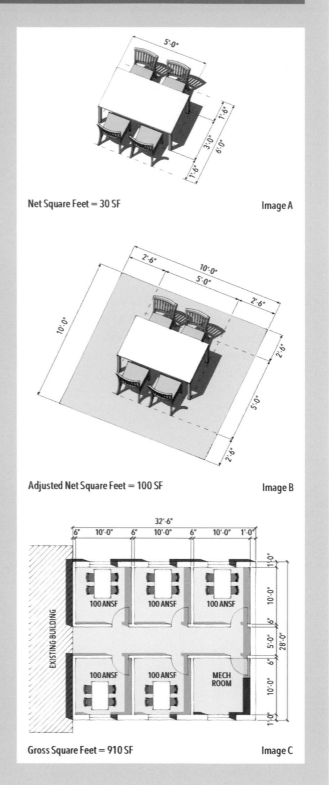

Net Square Feet = 30 SF   Image A

Adjusted Net Square Feet = 100 SF   Image B

Gross Square Feet = 910 SF   Image C

Figure 4.1. Understanding square feet

PRINT COLLECTIONS

Traditional Shelving

Figure 4.2. Traditional shelving in this small public library is filled to capacity, with very little empty space on the shelves for adjusting the collection.

Traditional upright DF shelving is the most common storage method (see figure 4.2). It is available in a variety of heights, and typically consists of a 2-inch wide upright with metal shelves on either side. The depth of these shelves varies, but typically, 11-inch-deep base shelves on each side of the upright creates a 24-inch-wide DF unit. With a minimum 36-inch-wide aisle between them, these shelves can be laid out most efficiently 5 feet on center. In academic general collections, it is not uncommon for the overall width of a DF unit to

be 18 inches, consisting of 2-inch uprights with 8-inch-deep shelves on either side. With a minimum 36-inch-wide aisle between them, these shelves can be laid out at 4 feet 6 inches on center. Likewise, DF units wider than 24 inches are sometimes used for certain oversized collections (see figure 4.3).

For planning purposes, 20 SF per DF unit is utilized. This number can be lower if narrower base shelves or a denser configuration is utilized; however, this number will increase if wider aisles are preferred or if alternative, nonorthogonal shelving arrangements are anticipated.

When using shelving units taller than 66 inches, seismic/lateral support must be addressed. This can become especially complicated on raised flooring, since many building codes require lateral loads to be transferred to the surrounding structure. If the load is to be transferred to the slab beneath a raised floor, undercarriages may need to be provided. This solution can be costly, make the shelving difficult to move, and defeats the inherent flexibility that a raised floor offers. Shelving heights of 66 inches or less can also be made more flexible through the introduction of casters to allow for spontaneous and easy rearranging by the library staff.

When considering rearranging existing shelving, it is important to determine whether the existing shelving is starter-adder or welded-frame shelving. Typically,

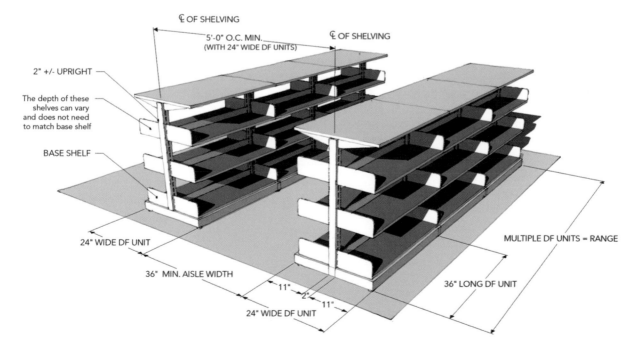

Figure 4.3. The image shows two ranges, comprised of three DF units each, spaced five feet on center to allow for a thirty-six-inch aisle. Each DF unit is twenty-four inches wide by thirty-six inches long. This arrangement represents the minimal spacing for twenty-four-inch wide shelving. Many libraries prefer wide aisles.

welded-frame shelving units can stand independently and be rearranged and reconfigured without any consideration for the number of ranges. With starter-adder shelving units, however, each individual range begins with a starter DF unit that has adder units attached to it. For example, if an existing library has ten ranges comprised of starter-adder shelving, those ranges cannot be reconfigured into fifteen shorter ranges without the addition of five new starter units. Determining what kind of shelving an existing library contains is an important first step in any Road Map. In either case, each type has advantages and disadvantages, and the benefits will vary depending on the manufacturer.

In summary, traditional shelving is common, affordable, and easily adjustable and browsable, but it is the least efficient in terms of the amount of space required per item stored.

Compact Shelving

Figure 4.4. Compact shelving eliminates aisles to increase storage capacity. Users are able to browse the collections as the ranges are opened.

Compact shelving is similar to traditional metal shelving, but the ranges move along metal tracks, allowing for the elimination of aisles between each range. The standard configuration groups several mobile ranges with space for only one aisle between two fixed ranges. The movable ranges slide to open an aisle between any two ranges in that group. This creates almost twice as much storage capacity as traditional metal shelving by eliminating all but one aisle in a group of ranges (see figure 4.4).

Because compact shelving can hold almost twice as much material as traditional metal shelving, the building structure must be designed for almost twice the weight. Most existing structures are not adequately designed for the heavy weight of this kind of shelving; therefore, in existing facilities, it is almost always limited to existing slab-on-grade conditions. Compact shelving can be either manually or electrically operated and comes with many safety features and programmable modes that can benefit special collections and archival storage facilities. Figure 4.5 reveals a case study in which one library used compact shelving on the ground level to consolidate its collection.

CASE STUDY: 160,000 SF ACADEMIC LIBRARY

This five-level 160,000 SF academic library houses its general collection, bound periodicals, and government documents on two floors in traditional 90"-high DF shelving. The existing collections, highlighted in images A and B, occupy 1,450 DF units in 23,900 SF on the ground and main levels.

During the programming step, a collection summary was developed to account for reductions and growth in the aforementioned collections. The collections summary revealed that the library would require a total of 2,200 DF shelving units– an addition of 750 DF shelves.

Compact shelving was recommended to be installed on the ground level in order to accommodate the consolidation and future growth of the existing collections currently located on the ground and main levels. The compact shelving provides approximately 2,200 DF units in fewer square feet than the existing collections currently occupy. Image C illustrates seven bays of compact shelving occupying only 19,115 SF on the ground level. The net result is more shelving in less space.

existing collection footprint	23,900 SF
compact shelving footprint	– 19,115 SF
gained usable area within library	4,785 SF

By consolidating the print collections into compact shelving, 4,785 SF becomes available within the library for other purposes, while an additional 750 DF shelves have been added to accommodate the library's projected collection growth. If this same square footage was added as an addition to the library or built as a new building, it could cost as much as $2 million. The additional square footage would also result in increased operational and maintenance costs for the library.

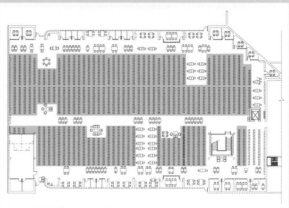

Image A. Existing Ground Level

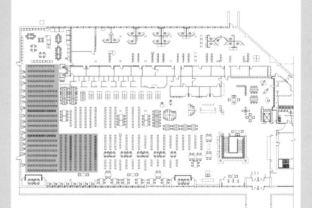

Image B. Existing Main Level

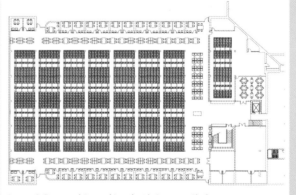

Image C. Proposed Ground Level with Compact Shelving

Figure 4.5. Compact shelving case study

High-Bay Storage

Figure 4.6. High-bay storage is an efficient use of space and common in repositories.

High-density storage facilities effectively house and preserve library materials while keeping these research tools readily accessible to library users. First developed at Harvard University in the mid-1980s, the high-bay storage approach uses best practices from the bulk storage industry, complete with a technologically advanced inventory control system. Books are arranged by size instead of classification code in order to maximize space, and therefore are not browsable by the user. Because of this, books are stored in large trays utilizing warehouse shelving that can be as high as 35 feet. This means that thousands of volumes can be stored in a relatively small footprint. Often referred to as the "Harvard Hi-Bay Approach," it has been adopted by more than a hundred libraries and has proven to be efficient, relatively inexpensive for storing print volumes, and easy to operate with a small staff component. This approach has long been used by Harvard Libraries, with approximately eight million volumes in storage (see figure 4.6).

Automated Storage Retrieval Systems

Figure 4.7. ASRS are the most efficient, but due to the high volume space required, they are most often incorporated into new library construction.

Automated storage and retrieval systems (ASRS) have become popular for extremely large collections within academic library settings. These require a large initial investment but offer many advantages over more traditional shelving options that are not as tall. The most significant advantage is their high-density storage capacity that can store more than twice as many books or other materials per square foot of floor area than high-bay storage systems. Additionally, these systems retrieve materials very quickly using automated computer-controlled technologies, and when located within the main library facility they can deliver items to patrons within minutes. The high-density storage efficiencies are gained through high-ceiling/volume spaces (as high as 50 feet) that are designed specifically to accommodate these systems, making them impractical for renovation or retrofit projects. They can, however, be incorporated into additions to existing libraries and used as a storage strategy in off-site repositories in which space is limited (see figure 4.7).

Off-Site Repositories

Another variable that should be mentioned in the discussion of storing collections is the ever-increasing use of off-site repositories to store collections—in part or in whole—in a remote location. This is a popular approach because it frees up square footage in an existing facility, it can be constructed for a fraction of the cost of a new or expanded library, and it can utilize one or more of the storage methods described above.

Summary

When determining the most appropriate storage strategy, it is helpful to understand the advantages and limitations of each. Figure 4.8 provides a comparative analysis of the different storage strategies. Which system is utilized will depend on several factors, including available space, capacity of existing structures, size of the collections, and cost.

SPECIAL COLLECTIONS AND ARCHIVES

Considerations

Special collections and archives (SCA) are found in both public and academic libraries but are more common in the latter. They generally consist of three main units: university archives, manuscripts, and collections of rare books, maps, broadsides, and other paper documents. These collections represent the unique primary source material valuable for original scholarship; they can be an important part of a library's donor relations program, attract grants, serve as building blocks for research, and highlight areas of excellence that set the library apart from other libraries.

Planning for SCA in the Road Map process is different because of the nature of the materials, their storage, and their use. Some of the primary considerations SCA spaces should take into account include:

- *Location:* Because of the nature of the collections, their inherent uniqueness, and their interest to a wide variety of users, SCA are sometimes placed in prime locations that can showcase an institution's treasures. Exhibit space is often located in, around, or adjacent to the SCA reading room, which often features upgraded carpets, ceiling and lighting, furnishings, and artwork that make it a showcase location for visitors.

- *Reading Room:* A sequestered reading room typically provides for supervised use of SCA materials, requiring it to be staffed when patrons are on-site. In preparing to work with a new patron, staff must register the patron in the database and provide rules for use of the collection, a storage space for personal items not allowed in the reading room, and copy or scanning equipment for image capture where allowed. The room is designed so that there are sightlines to all users from the main service desk.

- *Materials:* SCA contents and materials are usually stored in a remote location, often in the library building but sometimes elsewhere, which means that they must be paged/retrieved for use. Requirements for this vary but certainly include a user interface to make requests, generate pick lists for staff to retrieve materials, and track materials that are currently in use.

- *Donations:* Planning the capacity for storage of SCA materials can be difficult due to the unknowns surrounding potential future donations. Items acquired through budgeted acquisition funds on an annual basis are easy to project and plan for, but it is hard to estimate how many large collections the library might receive, and when it might receive them, over any given period of time. Additionally, because SCAs continue to grow, there is a sense in the Road Map planning process that no matter how much growth is projected, it will eventually not be enough. Balancing the desire to provide as much growth capacity as possible with what can be practically achieved in the Road Map can be a challenge. In light of this, high-density storage strategies are almost always considered whenever possible.

- *Environment:* SCA spaces are sometimes fitted with upgraded HVAC systems for better control of temperature and humidity, as well as special insulation, flooring, and lighting. These environmental qualities must also be compatible with the human physical needs of the staff. Furthermore, various items within the collections, such as film and digital materials, may require individual storage rooms with their own specific microclimates for their preservation.

In the Road Map process, careful attention should be given to the scope of the work needed to be done to existing systems of any particular area when

	STATISTICS	ADVANTAGES	DISADVANTAGES
TRADITIONAL 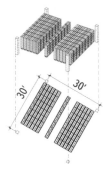	90"-High Metal Shelving 30' x 30' bay 48 DF units @ 42 LF/unit = 2,016 LF x 8 volumes/LF = 16,128 volumes / 900 SF = *18 VOL/SF*	1. The library usually has an ample supply of this type of shelving. 2. The look can be dramatically changed easily and inexpensively using new end panels and refinishing methods. 3. Existing libraries are usually designed to support loads for this shelving; it can be accommodated within existing ceiling heights.	1. It occupies the most space when housing a collection.
COMPACT 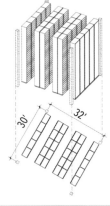	90"-High Compact Shelving 30' x 30' bay 104 DF units @ 42 LF/unit = 4368 LF x 8 volumes/LF = 34,944 volumes / 900 SF = *39 VOL/SF*	1. It takes up less floor area than traditional shelving to house the same size collection. 2. It is not necessarily limited to the 90" height. It can extend as high as 12' when utilized in a closed stack situation. 3. It can be installed on most slab-on-grade conditions by using elevated rails and ramps around the perimeter.	1. Its initial cost is expensive (but less than the cost of new construction). 2. It is heavier than traditional shelving and most elevated floors in existing libraries cannot support it. Therefore, it usually can only be located on slab-on-grade conditions or lowest level of an existing library.
HIGH BAY	35' Xtend High-Bay System 32' x 30' bay 30 units x 29 shelves/unit = 870 shelves x 18" LF/shelf = 15,660 LF x 8 volumes/LF = 125,280 volumes/960 SF = average of 6 "C" boxes *130 VOL/SF*	1. It can go much higher than the first two methods and can store even more volumes in a smaller footprint than traditional and compact shelving. 2. The existing tagging or coding of the materials can be utilized most of the time.	1. It is usually installed in new facilities and rarely in existing spaces due to height requirements. 2. It usually requires a motorized lift to access high bins. 3. It requires additional software, containers and shelving apparatus, and so on.
ASRS 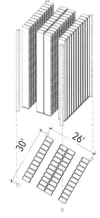	50' High Automated Library Storage System 26' x 30' bay 44 units x 49 bins/unit = 2156 bins x 10 LF/bin = 21,560 LF x 8 volumes/LF = 172,480 volumes / 780 SF = *221 VOL/SF*	1. It can be configured extremely high, more so than the first three methods. 2. Retrieval of an item is automated through the use of a robotic arm and inventory software program that is extremely fast and can have the item in the hands of a user within minutes if located near the service point. 3. Over time, the computer relocates highly circulated items closer to the staff work stations and makes their future retrieval even faster, while less frequently circulated items work their way to the outlying bins.	1. It is usually installed in new facilities and rarely in existing spaces due to the height requirements. 2. The initial cost is expensive, but can be offset by the need to build "less" building to house the collection.

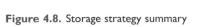

Figure 4.8. Storage strategy summary

investigating alternative locations for the SCA, to determine how best to meet their programmatic needs. Locating these spaces on upper levels directly under roofs or along exterior walls—where direct heat loads, humidity, and ultraviolet light can cause problems—should be avoided, and these are only a few of the factors that must be considered. Existing walls in older structure often do not contain adequate insulation to meet current building codes. In hot and humid climates, introducing especially cool environments to interior spaces along an exterior wall can lead to the formation of condensation within the wall, causing more problems.

Materials

The following is a brief overview of the main units of the SCA within the library. Different collections possess different storage needs, ranging from their required level of security and accessibility to their environmental conditions to the shape and size of their containers. Figure 4.9 provides an example of how archival storage boxes work better on shelving of a specific dimension that is different from that of traditional books. In a Road Map, the difference of a few inches in the size of storage shelving can have a large impact in terms of how a SCA area is organized.

University Archives

In the academic environment, the university archives (UA) department documents the history of the institution and often includes management of university records. In the latter instance, managers work with unit heads and legal counsel to institute retention and collecting policies across the university. UA departments are an important part of the institution's memory and traditions, and provide a useful cache of information with which to document changes over time. UA collections often provide important information that is of interest to researchers and can form the basis for outreach projects and support research across multiple disciplines. UA collections also provide a rich source of material for exhibits, articles in campus publications, development activities, and public relations events.

Manuscript Collections

Generally, manuscript collections contain unique and primary resource materials from the personal archives of scholars, authors, politicians, and others. A manuscript collection is typically made up of personal correspondence, private research documents such as diaries, and personal legal documents, including deeds or wills. They may consist of an author's early drafts of published materials, written notes, exchanges with editors or publishers, and other information about the publication process. A manuscript collection may also contain the business records of a company, including correspondence, product development documentation, and advertising and sales promotional items.

Rare Books

Any number of factors can lead to designation of a book as rare. Age is not always a factor, and neither is cost; rather, a panoply of characteristics can form a collection of rare books that is identified as exclusive, unusual, and deserving of closer scrutiny. Some have pointed out that with so much communication becoming digital, we may soon live in a world where all books are rare. This won't happen any time soon, based on what continues to be a robust publishing industry. For libraries, the physical allure of the rare book can be its graphic immediacy, vintage aesthetics, handmade craftsmanship, or importance as a historical artifact. Original-condition books printed more than one hundred years ago are prized because they display elements of book production: printing, binding, materials, and so on.

Summary

When developing a Road Map that includes SCA, it is important to evaluate the needs of the other SCA spaces required beyond those needed to store the collections. Such spaces include staff areas, workrooms, donation intake spaces, special project workrooms, staging areas, preservation labs, digitization spaces, display and exhibit areas, seminar and teaching spaces, and donor lounge and conference areas, as well as areas to host receptions and special events.

There are many other requirements and details that must be considered to make successful and functional SCA spaces, but in the context of developing a Road Map, the location of the SCA within the library, the spaces that are next to the SCA, and limitations and challenges of the existing structure and building presents are of prime importance. As with other spaces within the library, the details and specifics will be further developed during the final design of that particular space.

ARCHIVAL BOXES

Because archival spaces are usually defined by volume–that is, cubic feet of materials rather than linear feet due to the variety of formats and sizes of the items that comprise the collections– shelving and storage capacity are also calculated in terms of volume. The most common building block in calculating the storage capacity of an archival collection is the standard 12"W x 15"L x 10"H archival storage box, as shown in image A. While there are archival boxes of all shapes and sizes, this is the most common and forms the basis of the most efficient shelving layout. The volume within this box totals approximately 1 cubic foot of storage.

Rather than using traditional library shelving that holds books and measures between 18"-24"W x 36"L, it is slightly more efficient to shelve archival boxes on shelving with a footprint of 32"W x 40"L. A single shelf of this size will hold six archival boxes (see image B), with the label facing the aisle, but will accommodate larger, flatter archival boxes as well. It is not uncommon, however, to find libraries using regular book shelving to house archival boxes (see image C).

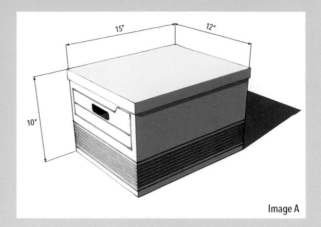

Image A

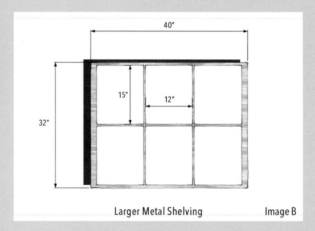

Larger Metal Shelving   Image B

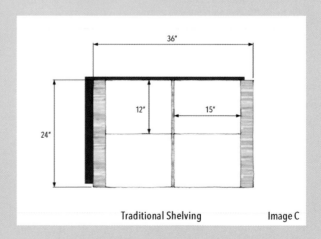

Traditional Shelving   Image C

Figure 4.9. Archival boxes

ANATOMY OF A LIBRARY BUDGET

BUDGETING FOR A LIBRARY PROJECT

Step 6 of the Road Map process, described in chapter 3, introduced the idea of the total project cost, which includes both the hard and the soft costs of the project. That chapter also described the process a consultant follows to develop an estimate for an individual phase, multiple phases, or the entire Road Map.

This chapter will provide greater detail and explanation of the categories that comprise the hard and soft costs that make up the total project cost, which is sometimes described as the *total project budget*. First, however, it is helpful to understand the concept of maintaining equilibrium among a project's cost, its quantity, and its quality.

Cost, Quantity, and Quality

The total project cost—a project's budget—must maintain equilibrium between three factors: cost, quantity, and quality, which are defined as:

Cost   The available funds for the project
Quantity   The scope of the project, in terms of SF and FF&E
Quality   The level of materials, finishes, and systems

Almost without exception, whether in a new library or a Road Map for an existing one, one of these items— and sometimes two—is fixed and the remaining ones must balance.

Example #1: The university administration wants to perform the work delineated in phase 1 of their Road Map, which encompasses the entire first floor, in order to improve the first impression given to prospective students and faculty. They state, "This is a priority; we need to know how much it will cost so we can find the money."

In this example the area, or *quantity*, of phase 1 is fixed; therefore, the *cost* for that phase is directly related to the *quality* of finishes and work to be done in that area. In other words, since the area of phase 1 is fixed, the nicer the renovation, the more is will cost. *Quality* and *cost* are directly proportional; if one increases, so does the other (see figure 5.1a).

Example #2: The friends of the library approach the library board of their public library and say, "We have raised $100,000; how much of the Road Map will that achieve?"

In this example the budget, or *cost*, is fixed; therefore, the amount, or *quantity*, of the Road Map that can be accomplished will depend on the *quality* of the finishes and systems provided. In this case, the quantity and quality are inversely proportional; if one increases, the other decreases (see figure 5.1b).

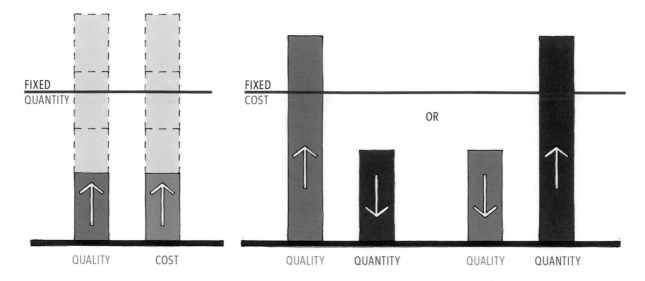

EXAMPLE A

With a fixed quantity, the cost increases as the quality of the work increases.

EXAMPLE B

With a fixed cost, the quantity decreases as the quality of the work increases and vice versa.

Figure 5.1. Cost, quality, and quantity

TOTAL PROJECT BUDGET

As stated earlier, the total project cost comprises both hard and soft costs, and step 6 of the Road Map process described in chapter 3 enumerates the actions used to estimate it. The total project budget is a planning tool that often precedes a project, and sometimes even a Road Map. Whether one starts with the size of the project to determine its cost or with the maximum allowable cost to determine the size, the total project budget is a useful tool and a reliable guide. It establishes mini-budgets for every hard- and soft-cost category and can be adjusted to reflect realistic and adequate expectations for each. It is created by identifying all the costs for each piece of the pie at the beginning and helps ensure that the project comes in, on, or under budget. Figure 5.2 is an example of a total project budget for a library project.

Total Project Budget

I.	**TOTAL ESTIMATED CONSTRUCTION COST**	(A + B)					**$0**
	A.	Construction Cost					
		a. New Construction/Addition(s)	0 GSF @	$1	per SF		$0
		b. Renovations	0 GSF @	$1	per SF		$0
	B.	Design Contingency					
		a.	0% of I.A				$0
II.	**TOTAL ESTIMATED FF&E**	(Fixtures, Furnishings and Equipment D.1–E.9)					**$0**
	D.1	Furniture	0 GSF @	$1	per SF		$0
	D.2	Shelving	0 GSF @	$1	per SF		$0
	D.3	Signage	0 GSF @	$1	per SF		$0
	E.1	Theft Detection/RFID System					$0
	E.2	Building Security System					$0
	E.3	Access Controls					$0
	E.4	Telephone System					$0
	E.5	Voice & Data Cabling					$0
	E.6	Audio Visual Equipment					$0
	E.7	Computer Hardware & Software					$0
	E.8	Specialized Library Equipment					$0
	E.9	Copiers					$0
	E.10	Other					$0
III.	**TOTAL ESTIMATED PROFESSIONAL COMPENSATION**	(F.1–F.5)					**$0**
	F.1	Pre-Design Services					
		a. Road Map					$0
		b. Feasibility Studies					$0
		c. Existing Facility Documentation					$0
		d. Programming					$0
		e. Other					$0
	F.2	Architecture and Engineering Basic Design Services					
		a.	0.00 of I. (Total Est. Construction Cost)				$0
	F.3	FF&E Design Services					
		a.	0.00 of II. (FF&E Costs)				$0
	F.4	Additional Services					
		a. Sustainability Consulting					$0
		b. Landscape Architecture					$0
		c. Civil Engineering & Permitting Services					$0
		d. Cost Estimating					$0
		e. Acoustic Consultant					$0
		f. Lighting Consultant					$0
		g. A/V, Technology, Low-Voltage Consultant					$0
		h. Security Consultant					$0
		i. Other					$0
	F.5	Reimbursable Expenses					
		a.					$0
IV.	**TOTAL ESTIMATED OWNER EXPENSES**	(G.1–G.3)					**$0**
	G.1	Pre-Design Phase Expenses					
		a. Land Acquisition Cost					$0
		b. Site Survey					$0
		c. Environmental Studies					$0
		d. Hazardous Material Assessments					$0
		e. Other					$0
	G.2	Design & Construction Phase Expenses					
		a. Geotechnical Testing					$0
		b. Special Inspections					$0
		c. Temporary Facility Expenses					$0
		d. Commissioning Agent					$0
		e. Construction Contingency	0% of I.A				$0
		f. Other					$0
	G.3	Post Construction Expenses					
		a. Library Materials					$0
		b. Moving Costs					$0
		c. Other					$0
V.	**TOTAL ESTIMATED PROBABLE PROJECT COST**						**$0**

Figure 5.2. Total project budget

Hard Costs

Figure 5.3 is an excerpt from the total project budget.

Total Project Budget

I.	TOTAL ESTIMATED CONSTRUCTION COST		(A + B)			$0
A.	Construction Cost					
	a. New Construction/Addition(s)	0 GSF @	$1	per SF		$0
	b. Renovations	0 GSF @	$1	per SF		$0
B.	Design Contingency					
	a.		0% of I.A			$0

Figure 5.3. I—Total estimated construction cost

Line I: Total Estimated Construction Cost (Totals Lines A and B)

LINE A: CONSTRUCTION COST

The construction cost is the amount of money paid to the contractor for his or her services to build the project. There are separate lines (a) for new construction and additions and (b) for renovations. Each line multiplies the gross square feet (GSF) of that portion of the project by an assumed cost per square foot for that work to arrive at a line total. (Someone unfamiliar with what the cost per square foot should be can find this number by asking a local architect or librarian who has recently completed a similar project.) If a project involves both new construction and renovation, both lines should be used because the cost per square foot for each would be different.

LINE B: DESIGN CONTINGENCY

The design contingency is an allowance set aside to cover increases and unexpected fluctuations in the costs of things like raw materials, labor, energy, and so on that may occur between the time the budget is established and the start of construction. These fluctuations can be caused by any number of circumstances, such as market and economic instability, natural disasters, or inflation, rendering the assumed cost per square foot assumptions in line A inadequate. The longer the period of time between the establishment of the budget and start of construction, the larger this contingency should be.

Soft Costs

Figure 5.4 is an excerpt from the total project budget. It is important to note that not every category listed under line II is included in every project. It is up to the owner to decide what systems are necessary and whether they should be included in the total project budget. Furthermore, many, if not most, of the categories listed under line II are provided and installed by the owner after the building construction is complete. When the owner provides these items after the building is constructed, it saves the owner money because the contractor would add a markup if he or she were responsible for the ordering, delivery, and installation of these items. This does require significant coordination, which is usually facilitated by the architect.

II.	TOTAL ESTIMATED FF&E	(Fixtures, Furnishings and Equipment D.1–E.9)				$0
D.1	Furniture	0 GSF @	$1	per SF		$0
D.2	Shelving	0 GSF @	$1	per SF		$0
D.3	Signage	0 GSF @	$1	per SF		$0
E.1	Theft Detection/RFID System					$0
E.2	Building Security System					$0
E.3	Access Controls					$0
E.4	Telephone System					$0
E.5	Voice & Data Cabling					$0
E.6	Audio Visual Equipment					$0
E.7	Computer Hardware & Software					$0
E.8	Specialized Library Equipment					$0
E.9	Copiers					$0
E.10	Other					$0

Figure 5.4. II—Total estimated FF&E

Line II: Total Estimated FF&E (Totals Lines D.1–E.9)

LINES D.1–D.3: FURNITURE, SHELVING, AND SIGNAGE

Lines D.1–D.3 include all the furniture, library shelving, and signage for the project. The amount of money allocated for each of these lines should take into account any specialty items, including the refinishing or reupholstering of existing furniture, display or compact shelving, and wayfinding, directional, end panel, and donor signage.

LINE E.1: THEFT DETECTION/RFID SYSTEM

The amount allocated to theft detection will depend on the type of system and equipment the library prefers, and should include automated material handling, self-checkout, and RFID equipment. Often a library RFID consultant can be engaged to help define the scope and cost for these systems, and sometimes the budget figure for this category is provided directly by the owner. If the library is moving to RFID for the first time as a result of this project, this number may also include the cost for retagging the existing collections.

LINE E.2: BUILDING SECURITY SYSTEM

The budget amount for building security is usually determined through the efforts of a security consultant or a security system vendor with whom the owner already has a relationship, and will depend on the type of system and options desired, including the number and types of cameras, the presence of intrusion detection, the amount of video recording storage provided, and so on. The rough-in (conduit and electrical boxes) and blocking in the walls to mount the equipment are provided as a part of the construction cost. This line is for the hardware, software, and installation of the security system only.

LINE E.3: ACCESS CONTROL SYSTEM

When included in a project's scope, access control systems often relate to and tie into the selected security system. This is a popular system that utilizes card swipe, keypad, or fob technologies in lieu of traditional keys, allowing access to different areas within the building to be controlled, limited, and managed using computer software. Access cards of those who are no longer employed by the library can be programmed to deny access immediately. These systems also allow the library to track and keep a record of which card opened which door at any particular time. When these systems incorporate the use of electronic strikes or magnetic locks integrated in the door hardware, those items are typically included in the construction cost as a part of the door hardware costs.

LINE E.4: TELEPHONE SYSTEM

The cost of the telephone system is another that is typically provided by the owner or established using the help of an IT consultant. When a VoIP system is utilized, much of this cost, including the handset devices, is included in the IT budget.

LINE E.5: VOICE AND DATA CABLING

The cost of voice and data cabling is based on the type of cabling, the number of drops, and the length of runs desired by the library. This is one category many libraries include in the construction cost so that the contractor is responsible for running the cable and testing it before it is turned over to the owner. Sometimes, however, owners like to have their preferred cabling vendors pull the wire.

LINE E.6: AUDIOVISUAL EQUIPMENT

The scope of audiovisual equipment required can range from a simple projection system and screen in a meeting room to full audiovisual capabilities throughout the library, including room reservation systems, flat-screen monitors with video conferencing, public announcement systems, digital media studios, A/V recording studios, visualization labs, and so on. The budget figures for this category are almost always developed through close collaboration between the library staff, architect, electrical engineer, and an A/V design consultant. Often these systems are closely related to and can impact the decisions made regarding the type of cabling, hardware, and software specified and budgeted in lines E.5 and E.7.

LINE E.7: COMPUTER HARDWARE AND SOFTWARE

The budget number for computer hardware and software is most often provided by the library, which is usually well versed in the purchase and cost of new computer hardware and software. However, many libraries rely on IT consultants to help determine the detailed specifications for IT hardware such as computers, tablets, online public access catalogs, computer training room systems, wireless devices, printers, laptops, servers, racks, routers, switches, and so on.

LINE E.8: SPECIALIZED LIBRARY EQUIPMENT

Specialized library equipment includes such items as microfilm reader printers, DVD cleaning and repair equipment, archival copiers and scanners, people counters, sight and hearing assistive technologies, and so on. The budget number for this line is usually provided by the library.

LINE E.9: COPIERS

If copiers are to be purchased, this budget category should reflect the number and type desired. Sometimes copiers are leased and are funded through yearly operating budgets instead of the total project budget. In either case, decisions on the type, number, and options to be provided (such as color printing and scanning) should be made in light of the decisions made in many of the categories above.

LINE E.10: OTHER

Line E.10 and subsequent lines (if needed) can be used for other systems or equipment. An example of other equipment to be budgeted might include kitchen equipment for culinary teaching kitchens or café components. Other lines might include specialty literacy and educational equipment, playground equipment, and so on. The library should feel free to add additional lines to be sure that all known expenses are identified and included in the total project budget.

Line III: Total Estimated Professional Compensation (Totals Lines F.1–F.5)

LINE F.1: PRE-DESIGN SERVICES

Line F.1 is budgeted for fees and expenses that may be incurred by the owner prior to the commencement of the actual design and construction of a project or phase of a Road Map. Often the owner may need to pay for preliminary studies and planning exercises to help bring definition to a project. A Road Map is an example of a pre-design service.

LINE F.2: ARCHITECTURAL AND ENGINEERING BASIC DESIGN SERVICES

Architectural and engineering (A&E) basic design services include architect's design services and engineering services that include mechanical, electrical, plumbing, fire protection, structural, and sometimes civil engineering. These services include the design of the building, production of contract (bid) documents, management of the bidding process, and monitoring the construction phase.

Establishing the budget for the A&E basic design services fee usually begins by multiplying a percentage fee by the construction cost in line A. The percentage used in this calculation varies and is sometimes dictated by institutions or governmental agencies. The general rule of thumb is the smaller the project, the higher the percentage fee, which can range anywhere from 6 percent for large projects to 15 percent or more for very small projects and will vary depending on the project's complexity and schedule.

III. TOTAL ESTIMATED PROFESSIONAL COMPENSATION (F.1–F.5)		$0
F.1	Pre-Design Services	
	a. Road Map	$0
	b. Feasibility Studies	$0
	c. Existing Facility Documentation	$0
	d. Programming	$0
	e. Other	$0
F.2	Architecture and Engineering Basic Design Services	
	a. 0.00 of I. (Total Est. Construction Cost)	$0
F.3	FF&E Design Services	
	a. 0.00 of II. (FF&E Costs)	$0
F.4	Additional Services	
	a. Sustainability Consulting	$0
	b. Landscape Architecture	$0
	c. Civil Engineering & Permitting Services	$0
	d. Cost Estimating	$0
	e. Acoustic Consultant	$0
	f. Lighting Consultant	$0
	g. A/V, Technology, Low-Voltage Consultant	$0
	h. Security Consultant	$0
	i. Other	$0
F.5	Reimbursable Expenses	
	a.	$0

Figure 5.5. III—Total estimated professional compensation

LINE F.3: FF&E DESIGN SERVICES

Usually the selection and specifying of interior finishes—that is, colors and materials—is included in the basic services fee in line F.2. Line F.3 covers the fees associated with the design, selection, specifying, procurement, and installation of the furniture, shelving, and signage in lines D.1–D.3

LINE F.4: ADDITIONAL SERVICES

Additional services are fees paid to the architect for services provided by engineers and consultants for work that is not included in the A&E basic design services. Additional services fees usually correlate to the equipment budgets listed in Lines E.1–E.10, but also include fees for services such as landscape architecture, cost estimating, and so on. Other additional services fees might include, for example, the work of traffic or kitchen consultants.

LINE F.5: REIMBURSABLE EXPENSES

Reimbursable expenses include travel, meals, postage, printing, and other miscellaneous expenses for the architect, interior designer, engineers, and specialty consultants.

Line IV: Total Estimated Owner Expenses (Totals Lines G.1–G.3)

LINE G.1: PRE-DESIGN PHASE EXPENSES

Line G.1 budgets for the owner's potential administrative costs that might occur during the pre-design phase. In new projects, costs related to securing property—including the land purchase, environmental studies, and survey work—may be required. In renovations of existing buildings and Road Maps, owners will need to verify the presence of hazardous materials such as asbestos and lead paint. If they are present, the owner will have to abate those materials prior to the work or incorporate abatement into the overall scope of work.

LINE G.2: DESIGN AND CONSTRUCTION PHASE EXPENSES

Line G.2 budgets for owner expenses—such as geotechnical testing, special inspections, commissioning, and so on—that occur during the design and construction of the project. A geotechnical report is needed for new projects to establish the criteria for the design of the building's foundation, which can be done only after the location for the building on the site is established. During the construction process, building codes require that the design team identify the inspection of certain components of the building. The hiring of a commissioning agent is required by certain sustainability rating systems to provide independent testing to confirm that the building systems have been installed and operate as designed.

One of the most important expense lines in this section is the construction contingency. This contingency is an allowance set aside to cover change orders that arise during the construction phase, including changes resulting from unforeseen conditions, code-related adjustments, minor design team errors in the drawings, and changes in the work initiated by the owner. These are essentially reserve

IV. TOTAL ESTIMATED OWNER EXPENSES (G.1–G.3)				$0
G.1	Pre-Design Phase Expenses			
	a. Land Acquisition Cost		$0	
	b. Site Survey		$0	
	c. Environmental Studies		$0	
	d. Hazardous Material Assessments		$0	
	e. Other		$0	
G.2	Design & Construction Phase Expenses			
	a. Geotechnical Testing		$0	
	b. Special Inspections		$0	
	c. Temporary Facility Expenses		$0	
	d. Commissioning Agent		$0	
	e. Construction Contingency	0% of I.A	$0	
	f. Other		$0	
G.3	Post Construction Expenses			
	a. Library Materials		$0	
	b. Moving Costs		$0	
	c. Other		$0	
V. TOTAL ESTIMATED PROBABLE PROJECT COST				$0

Figure 5.6. IV—Total estimated owner expenses

funds held by the owner and are not part of the contract; they are used at the discretion of the owner in consultation with the architect. Most often, funds remaining in these contingencies at the end of construction can be used to fund other categories as necessary.

LINE G.3: POST-CONSTRUCTION EXPENSES

Post-construction expenses include the activities to make the building ready after the contractor is finished with construction. This category can include expenses such as donor appreciation events, ribbon-cutting ceremonies, and grand opening events. Another example might be moving the existing collection from the old location to the new one.

Line V: Total Estimated Probable Project Cost

Line V represents the grand total for the project budget.

6

GETTING STARTED

WHERE TO BEGIN

Once a library is convinced that making the most of its existing space is better than just making do, the process of funding a Road Map and getting a consultant on board may take months or even years. In the interim is an opportunity to take a step back and objectively evaluate the existing library's use of space. This can be challenging and requires discipline; however, there are things that can be done to make an immediate impact and are relatively easy to implement. These steps demonstrate a commitment to being more efficient and help prepare for the more global evaluation of the library's space during the Road Map process. Taking initial action will expedite the Road Map's implementation and simultaneously cultivate a visionary mentality and encourage outside-the-box thinking among the staff.

As requests for funding and procuring a Road Map work their way through the institution's protocol, the following steps should be considered to identify initial opportunities for improvement.

Clean House

Figure 6.1. Storage spaces like these need to be sorted to determine what can be discarded. The remaining items should be organized in an efficient manner.

For some, it is hard to throw away anything, but when staff members have to lean on storage room doors to close them and the closets and corners of the library look like those in figure 6.1, it is time for spring cleaning—no matter what month it is.

If something has not been touched in six months or more, throw it away, donate it, or surplus it. Schedule a staff workday and rent a Dumpster. Make it a contest to see which department can get rid of the greatest number of unneeded items. Don't wait for a consultant to come on board and develop a Road Map with spring cleaning as its first step; go ahead and get this out of the way. If you are prone to being a pack rat, designate and empower a two- or three-person committee to make final decisions about what to keep. Then let the rest go.

Evaluate the Collections

Figure 6.2. Remember, five empty DF shelves are equivalent to one small group study room.

Begin discussions on how to manage the print collections. Identify what can be weeded or deaccessioned, address duplicates, determine what can be accessed in perpetuity through online databases, and assess what has not been touched in years. Consider which items can be acquired through interlibrary loan or other channels in the rare instances they are requested. Librarians usually remember when items were originally purchased and the large amounts of money spent on them, which can make it hard to part with them. Again, empower those without an emotional attachment to weigh in and be the voice of reason. Remember that libraries are evolving to be more than repositories. Figure 6.2 is a reminder that each empty DF unit represents 20 SF of potential.

Because managing a collection and weeding select items is an enormous and time-consuming project, it is important to get an early start and be methodical.

Identify and Take Advantage of Underutilized Wall Space

Many libraries do not take advantage of open wall space. When collections can be repositioned to single-faced (SF) shelving along a wall, the floor area can be opened up for other uses. The example in figure 6.3 illustrates a periodical area in a university library. In this case, as with many libraries, the number of titles actually shelved had reduced substantially in recent years and the periodical shelving was less than half full. The images also indicate empty wall space between the windows along the perimeter. This example reveals how the space could be reconfigured with SF shelving along the walls to accommodate the remaining titles, freeing up the floor area for other purposes.

A View toward stacks

B View along wall

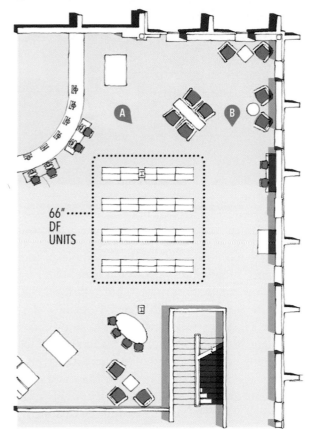

Image A

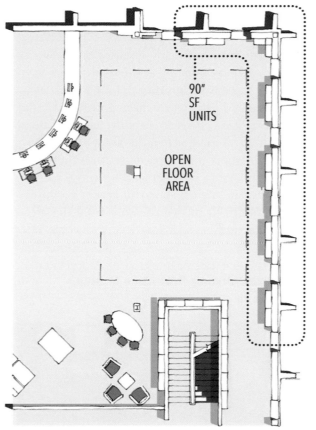

Image B

EXISTING FLOOR PLAN

The current shelving configuration utilizes 20 DF shelving units for the periodical collection. Each DF unit has three shelves per side for a total of 120 three-foot shelves. The shelves are less than half full; therefore, 60 shelves is sufficient to house the collection.

POTENTIAL FLOOR PLAN

By utilizing SF shelving along the perimeter walls for the periodical collection, 11 SF units with six shelves per side can be used for a total of 66 three-foot shelves. This is more than the 60 shelves needed to house the collection. The result is an open area that can be repurposed to meet other programmatic needs.

Figure 6.3. Underutilized wall space

Identify and Repurpose Underutilized Space That May Exist

Figure 6.4. These are images from a library that was preparing to undergo a planning exercise to create more room for new services. This space was underutilized but was not located where the additional space was needed.

It is counterintuitive, but many libraries that seem to have no room and are bursting at the seams often have areas in which space is underutilized. In these instances the library usually lacks space where it is needed and space is underutilized where it is not needed. The Road Map will address all the space in the library holistically; however, in the short term, spaces such as those pictured in figure 6.4 can be leveraged for more seating, technology, displays, or collaborative space. Try to use these opportunities to relieve pressure from the areas that are overstressed.

Identify Where Wrong Furniture Is Being Used and Fix It

Figure 6.5. Using furniture in ways for which it was not designed is inefficient and often unsightly.

Libraries are notorious for holding on to things—especially furniture that has outlived its purpose, such as old index tables and wooden card catalog cabinets. Often these pieces of furniture are repurposed to accommodate newer technologies or new types of media; however, reusing this furniture can sometimes result in an inefficient use of space. The table pictured in figure

6.5 is much deeper than required for the two desktop computers it holds, and it lacks an appropriate cable management system. New computer tables with appropriate cable management systems could hold four computers in nearly the same footprint this table occupies.

Figure 6.6. Existing oversized workstation

Figure 6.6 illustrates another example of inefficient furniture. In this case, however, it is not older furniture that is incorrectly repurposed, but rather relatively new furniture used in ways different from how it was designed. These workstations—used as study carrels in an academic library setting—are 6 feet wide by 6 feet long, occupying more area than four standard carrels. As this library worked through its Road Map and eliminated inefficiencies like these, planners were able to add 463 student seats to the seating within the existing library.

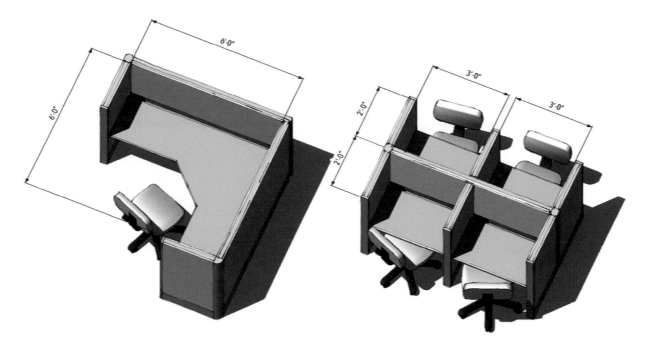

EXISTING WORKSTATION

The existing workstation occupies 36 SF for one seat. It provides ample individual study space; however, in a library that needs more seats, this option is inefficient.

STANDARD LIBRARY CARREL

The existing workstation is replaced with standard library carrels that can occupy the same amount of space. In student focus groups, students said they did not mind standard library carrels if equipped with power.

Figure 6.7. Workstation comparison

Declutter Work Areas to Increase Efficiency

Figure. 6.8. Messy work areas will impede the efficient workflow and processes that will benefit the staff and users.

In many libraries where there is no more room for storage, things begin to accumulate in general work areas as well as in staff offices and at individual workstations. Figure 6.7 illustrates this phenomenon. Sometimes clutter results when there is not enough work space in the library, and storage rooms are converted into staff work areas as a last resort. Either way, the result is the same: inefficient work areas that impede the staff's ability to efficiently do their work and serve the community.

Where space is at a premium, it is important to declutter as much as possible to free up valuable work space, perhaps as part of the spring cleaning process. Everything should have a place, and work surfaces should not be used to store items.

MOVING FORWARD WITH A ROAD MAP

Private organizations are usually able to move forward with great flexibility regarding decisions about how and who they hire, and how much they pay. A public institution's decision to move forward with a Road Map, however, usually involves several steps, almost always requiring input from administrative personnel and adherence to certain institutional procurement policies.

Some institutions allow the hiring of professional services without a formal request for qualifications (RFQ) or request for proposal (RFP) process if the total contract value is under a certain threshold; others require a formal selection process in every case. When a formal selection process is required, it is almost always prescribed and fairly inflexible.

RFQ versus RFP

RFQs and RFPs are both used to solicit professional services when a formal selection process is required, and both provide a detailed overview of the project scope and the desired services. Both also typically provide dates and deadlines for consultant questions to be submitted, indicating when owner answers will be provided, when the consultant's final submissions are due, and designated times for responders to tour the existing facility. Both RFQs and RFPs ask responders to provide their qualifications; however, an RFP asks each responder to also provide a detailed fee proposal to do the work, while an RFQ does not.

An RFQ usually asks consultants to present their qualifications by describing their approach and methodology and demonstrating the expertise of their team members and experience with similar projects or clients. Based on these criteria, the owner selects the most qualified consultant. This is known as a *qualification-based selection process* and is recommended by the American Institute of Architects. Once the preferred consultant is chosen, the scope of services and corresponding fee for the project is then negotiated.

When choosing to use an RFP, the owner must know exactly what the scope of work will entail, the specific services and deliverables the chosen consultant will provide, and a definitive schedule and deadline for completion of services. Often the RFP dictates a format that responders must use when submitting their fee proposals to help ensure an "apples-to-apples" comparison of fees. RFPs are popular and often used by owners when the fee is a primary consideration in the selection of a consultant.

If an RFP is chosen for use in the selection of a consultant, the following considerations should be kept in mind:

- Where there is ambiguity or a lack of clarity in the RFP's scope of work and project description, responders will make assumptions and resort to guesswork in formulating their fee proposals. This can make apples-to-apples comparisons difficult.

Unfortunately for the owner—and the consultants—this can lead to disparities between the fee proposals, and a well-qualified responder may be eliminated because his or her fee was higher due to a mistaken assumption. Even worse, the owner may never realize this is what happened.

- It has been said that "you don't know what you don't know." Sometimes the detailed description of the scope of work, desired services, and deliverables included in the RFP does not account for beneficial processes or services a consultant may offer because the owner did not know they existed. One way to avoid this is to allow a place in the fee proposal for the consultant to describe other recommended services and list the corresponding fees separately so that the apples-to-apples base fee is not skewed.

- It is important to recognize that evaluating and selecting a consultant solely on the basis of the lowest fee may eliminate a highly qualified—or the *most* qualified—and capable consultant. While most consultants will agree to negotiate and adjust their fees, scope, effort, and deliverables to accommodate an owner's budget, many RFP selection processes do not allow for this.

- Some states' architectural licensing and registration laws prohibit architects from quoting fees in the pursuit of work. This might make it difficult or preclude capable architects from proposing on a project even though they have relevant experience to offer. Owners can verify if this is the case by checking with their individual state's architectural licensing registration board.

The Selection Process

After receiving the responders' submissions to the RFQ or RFP, a selection committee—usually comprised of representative stakeholders in the project—will decide on their preferred candidate, and, if allowed, may award the project. Most often, however, the committee will formulate a short list of three or four top candidates and invite them to participate in face-to-face interviews with the committee to further discuss each consultant's proposals and qualifications.

Interviews are an effective way for owners to get to know the short-listed consultants, be introduced to the team who will actually be doing the work, ask detailed questions and seek clarification on the consultants' submissions, and learn more about each consultant's process and methodology. It is not uncommon for owners to prefer one consultant after reviewing the proposals and end up selecting someone else after interacting with the consultants during the interview process.

Keep in mind, however, that preparing for and attending an interview is an expensive endeavor for a consultant. It involves many hours of preparation and money for travel expenses to tour existing facilities and participate in the interview itself. Out of respect for the short-listed consultants and their investment of time and money, it is important to not shortchange the process with twenty-to-thirty-minute interviews in which very little information can be gleaned.

It is also not fair to the remaining short-listed consultants if the interview process is only a pretense to select a consultant everyone already wanted simply to fulfill procurement requirements. If an owner has a relationship with or simply wants to work with a particular consultant, there is nothing wrong with contacting that consultant alone, asking for a proposal, and moving forward with him or her if the institution's procurement policies allow. This will save an enormous amount of time, money, and energy. In fact, most consultants would rather this happen than spend time participating in the full process if they never really had a chance to begin with.

Ideally, interviews should last between an hour and an hour and a half to allow sufficient time for presentations, questions, and answers. It is during this dialogue that some of the most valuable information is exchanged. Effective consultant interviews typically include the following elements:

- *Introductions (3–5 mins.):* Introductions should be made by those representing the owner and the consultant.
- *Qualifications/Relevant Experience (5–10 mins.):* This should be a *short* review of the consultant's qualifications and relevant experience. However, since this information was previously included in the consultant's submission to the RFQ or RFP, the time spent on this in the interview should only highlight *why* and *how* what is presented is relevant to the owner's project.
- *Approach and Methodology (12–15 mins.):* The consultant should explain and demonstrate how he or she will approach the project and how his or her methodology involves the owner, community, and stakeholders in each step. It is important to have a clear understanding of the consultant's expectations for the owner's role in the process.

- *Insight (20–30 mins.):* This time should be spent talking about the owner's project, and should consequently be where the consultant spends the majority of his or her time in the presentation. The consultant should share insights, thoughts, challenges, and potential opportunities he or she has identified or believes exist through his or her past experience or familiarity with the owner's current situation. This is an opportunity for the owner to ascertain whether the consultant has a true grasp of the project's scope. Sometimes, consultants may offer ideas and concepts to try to impress a committee, demonstrate their creativity, or convey commitment and enthusiasm. For consultants there are pros and cons to this strategy, but owners should keep a sober mind and try to see beyond beautiful imagery and look for substance.
- *Q&A (20–30 mins.):* Time should be designated for questions and answers throughout and during the presentation. The owner should have ample opportunity to seek clarification and follow up on anything discussed in the presentation. Additionally, selection committees usually prepare a set of standard questions they ask every short-listed consultant as a way of gathering consistent information and comparing the consultants' responses.

During and immediately following the interviews, the selection committee usually ranks the presentations based on predetermined criteria to establish who is the highest-scoring consultant.

If the interviews are a part of a RFQ process, shortly thereafter, the highest-scoring consultant is asked to submit a fee proposal and enters into contract and fee negotiations with the owner. While this rarely happens, if mutually acceptable contract terms and a fee cannot be agreed upon, the owner has the option to move to the second-highest-scoring consultant and repeat the process until a fee and contract terms are agreed upon.

In the RFP selection process, owners sometimes require consultants to submit their proposed fee in a separate envelope that remains unopened until after the interviews are complete. Many owners believe that consultants who know that their proposed fees will be a part of the scoring criteria will keep them competitive. By not opening the envelopes until after the interviews, the short-listing of consultants is determined by qualifications alone. While the selection committee is not initially swayed by fees alone, the consultant's proposed fees do become one of the scoring criteria considered.

Once all the selection criteria are considered and the highest-scoring consultant is selected, the submitted fee becomes the basis for the fee negotiation. Once the fee and contract terms have been agreed upon and a contract signed, work can begin.

Consultant Qualities

Chemistry

The need for a consultant to possess expertise and experience is obvious. The next most important quality—chemistry—may be less so. It is important for the owner to ascertain whether he or she is compatible with the consultant. Can the owner envision working closely with the consultant over a long period? The fact is, the two will work closely together, and the synergies between them will play a large part in the Road Map's overall success.

Involvement

Understanding who will actually be doing the work and what their involvement will be throughout the Road Map process is important and sometimes difficult to determine. The consultant's explanation of his or her approach and methodology can help, but the owner should ask specific questions such as: Who will be on the consultant's team? Who will be my day-to-day contact? When in the process will the lead consultant be on-site? It is not uncommon for a consultant's principal or business development person to play a major role in an interview, so it is important to know if the people in the interview will be the ones doing the work.

Architect or Not?

Should the author of a Road Map be an architect? That is a common question librarians ask. Road Maps involve tasks that have been performed by traditional library consultants, such as developing building programs and performing management studies, but also require the skills of an architect who understands existing building systems and how to develop cost estimates, and so on. Because of the need for both skill sets, it is not uncommon for someone with deep knowledge of libraries to align him- or herself with someone who understands the architectural and planning process. Teaming arrangements designed to bring the necessary expertise together in hopes of being selected to author a Road Map can be successful, but the owner should ask questions such as:

- Have the members of the team successfully collaborated in the past? What were the challenges?
- Who on the team will be the prime contract holder and who will be the owner's day-to-day contact?
- Will communication with the team's library expert have to go through the contract holder? Can the owner talk to anyone on the team as needed?
- If members of the team disagree, who makes the final decision?

These are not questions regarding past experience or expertise; they are procedural in nature. Understanding how such a teaming arrangement will work and its impact on the owner's ability to collaborate with the team members doing the work is what must be clear.

7

CASE STUDIES

The case studies in this chapter offer examples of Road Maps for both small and large public and academic libraries. These case studies involve real libraries with real issues whose leaders recognized their library's inability to meet the needs of their respective communities and chose to do something about it, even though none had any identified funds to implement change.

Rather than do nothing while waiting for funding, these libraries sought to address their current inadequacies, define their future, and plot a course to get there. Each case study provides a summary of the context that led to the decision to author a Road Map. Existing floor plans are provided that include explanations of the challenges and shortcomings identified in the assessment step; proposed floor plans that explain the conceptual design solutions developed in concert with the library's input.

Following each case study's comparative explanations of the existing and proposed plans is a table that summarizes and quantifies measurable data to demonstrate the increased capacity of particular programmatic elements deemed important by the library's leadership. Finally, a phasing plan is included for each case study that enumerates the sequence of steps to be followed to transform the current library into the proposed solution presented.

The case studies range from an 8,000-square-foot public branch library to a 300,000-square-foot academic library. Regardless of the type and size of the facility, the process to develop each Road Map was the same. In every example, an increase in capacity, efficiency, and functionality was achieved within the existing walls of the structure. While this is not always the case with Road Maps, the examples selected demonstrate the potential for improvement inherent in every library given thoughtful consideration and careful prioritization of the issues at hand.

CASE STUDY 1

8,000-SQUARE-FOOT PUBLIC LIBRARY

8,000 SQUARE-FOOT PUBLIC BRANCH LIBRARY

PROJECT STATEMENT

The branch library moved into its current location in 1937, in what was a small 3,530 SF traditional rectangular building. In 1981, a precast concrete addition was constructed to increase the library's total square footage to approximately 8,000 SF. In 2012, the library board elected to move forward with a library Road Map to address several inadequacies and concerns.

PROJECT OBJECTIVES

The primary concerns and objectives to be addressed in the Road Map included the following:

- Address the existing help desk position–the librarian's back currently faces the door

- Add a second exit, or "escape route," from the public area

- Separate the local history/genealogy area from the adjacent children's picture book area

- Relocate the adult computers from the far wall, to a more convenient location for staff help and supervision

- Increase the usable square footage in the children's area and remove the general storage items located in the shelving aisles (see figure 6.1)

- Increase seating throughout the library

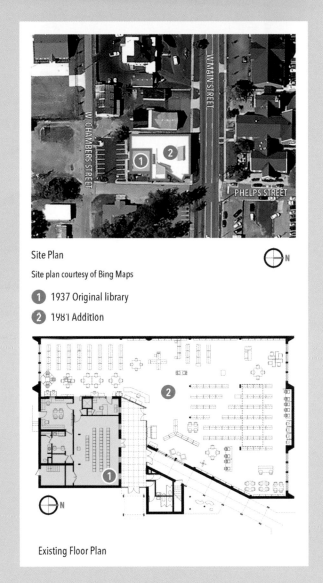

Site Plan

Site plan courtesy of Bing Maps

1 1937 Original library

2 1981 Addition

Existing Floor Plan

Figure 7.1. Case Study 1: Title sheet

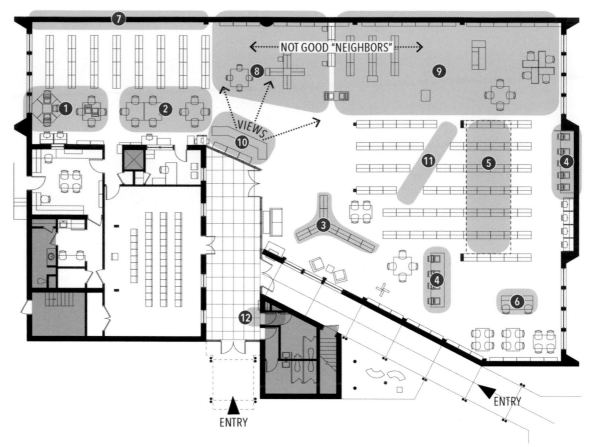

EXISTING MAIN LEVEL ⊕N

PLAN NOTES

1. Children's computers are crowded and not ADA accessible, and there is no room for parents and strollers.

2. Children's area is crowded and cluttered with miscellaneous furniture.

3. Low 42" periodical shelving configuration is inefficient.

4. Adult computers are segregated; there are not enough power outlets to have all of the computers located in a single location.

5. Roof monitor windows provide high-quality northern light and is currently blocked by 90" stacks.

6. Index table is unused.

7. Wall space is underutilized.

8. Picture book area with mural on wall.

9. Reference and local history area.

10. Orientation of the existing help desk does not give librarians a direct view of the library entrance.

11. Aisle space is inefficient.

12. Entry to toilets is not visible from the help desk.

Figure 7.2. Case Study 1: Existing main level

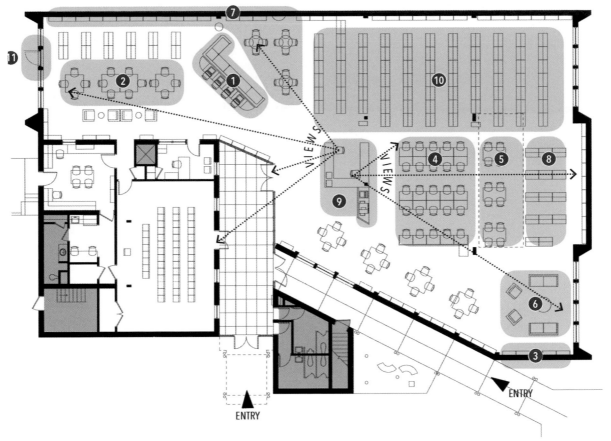

PROPOSED MAIN LEVEL ⊕N

PLAN NOTES

1. Additional children's computers are provided, and are now ADA accessible.

2. Additional furniture added to children's area; furniture is reconfigured and efficiently organized.

3. Periodicals collection is consolidated on 90" SF shelving.

4. Adult computers are located adjacent to help desk and print release station.

5. Roof monitor windows provide high quality northern light over study tables.

6. Index table is removed and replaced with soft lounge seating.

7. Picture book area is expanded; existing mural is retained.

8. Reference and local history area is relocated away from picture book area.

9. Centralized help desk provides maximum views of the library, including the entrance.

10. Adult fiction and nonfiction collections are positioned to buffer the picture book area from the adult areas.

11. An additional emergency exit is provided to address the owner's concern about providing adequate escape routes.

Figure 7.3. Case Study I: Proposed main level

PROJECT SUMMARY

MEASURABLES

	EXISTING	NEW	DIFFERENCE	PERCENT
DF UNITS	96	99	+3	3% INCREASE
STUDY TABLES	5	7	+2	40% INCREASE
CHILDREN'S SEATS	14	35	+21	150% INCREASE
COMPUTERS	8	25	+17	212% INCREASE
ADULT LOUNGE	2	6	+4	200% INCREASE

PHASING OVERVIEW

The following diagrams illustrate the phasing plans developed for the library to implement the proposed Road Map. There are three phases, and each centers around using the community meeting room as "swing" space where furniture, materials, and services are temporarily located while phased construction occurs in the library's public space.

OWNER'S STATEMENT

" There were no funds for new construction, and no interest by community and political leaders, except the Friends, in building a new library. There was, however, a strong need for a reconfigured, more appropriate, flexible use of space. We were able to leverage a small amount of state MRR (maintenance, renovation, and repair) money and some renovation funds provided by the Friends to create and implement the Road Map. The staff, leadership, and Friends responded well to the idea of a Road Map, and were delighted when the architect pointed out an existing ceiling monitor that let in natural daylight, but was never noticed due to the position of the existing tall shelving directly beneath it. "

–Carrie C. Zeiger
Regional Library Director (Retired), Flint River Regional Library System

PHASE 1

Phase 1 clears out the northeast corner by relocating materials and furniture in this area to the community meeting room.

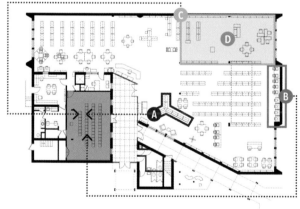

EXISTING MAIN LEVEL

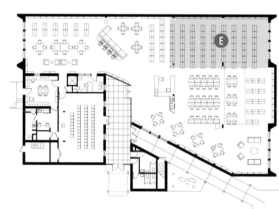

PROPOSED MAIN LEVEL

A Relocate the periodicals collection to SF shelving in the community room, shaded in gray. Remove the existing periodicals shelving in the public area.

B Relocate the existing computers to community room.

C Relocate the existing collection to the community room.

D In the highlighted area, renovate finishes, electrical, and lighting.

E Install new shelving arrangement. Relocate the adult collections to their final locations.

Figure 7.4. Case Study 1: Project summary

PHASE 2

The shaded gray regions represent areas renovated in previous phases. Phase 2 clears out and renovates the children's area.

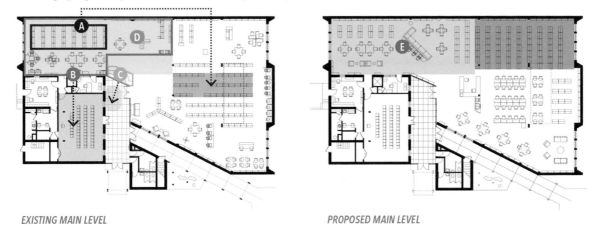

EXISTING MAIN LEVEL   *PROPOSED MAIN LEVEL*

Ⓐ Relocate the juvenile collection to a temporary location in previously emptied adult shelving.

Ⓑ Move children's area, including picture books and seating, to temporary location in community meeting room.

Ⓒ Relocate circulation desk to temporary location in lobby.

Ⓓ Renovate finishes, electrical, and lighting.

Ⓔ Install new shelving and furniture; relocate children's and juvenile collections and seating to their final locations.

PHASE 3

The shaded gray regions represent areas renovated in previous phases. Phase 3 renovates the balance of the library.

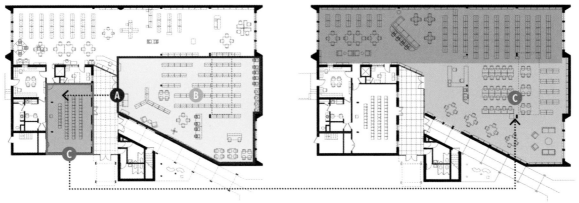

EXISTING MAIN LEVEL   *PROPOSED MAIN LEVEL*

Ⓐ Relocate remaining items to temporary location in the community meeting room.

Ⓑ Renovate balance of public space.

Ⓒ Move into newly renovated space.

Figure 7.5. Case Study 1: Phasing plans

CASE STUDY 2

25,000-SQUARE-FOOT ACADEMIC LIBRARY

25,000 SQUARE-FOOT ACADEMIC LIBRARY

PROJECT STATEMENT

This college was founded in 1900 as a small boarding school in a village in the North Carolina Blue Ridge Mountains. The library occupies the upper two levels of a three-story academic building. The two library levels have no restrooms; students are required to exit the library and travel to the lower level to use the facilities. Internally, the library houses a large print collection and lacks the infrastructure for current technology and student collaboration space.

PROJECT OBJECTIVES

The primary concerns and objectives to be addressed in the Road Map master plan included the following:

- Reduce the size of the print collection in response to online digital resources

- Add restroom facilities on both library levels

- Make the one elevator in the building accessible to the public space and compliant with ADA standards

- Add food service to the library

- Add small group study rooms and seminar rooms that can be used for presentations

- Increase the number of computers

- Provide a designated quiet study space

- Add active learning classrooms

- Increase staff work space

- Create a designated special collections and archives space

Site Plan

Site plan courtesy of Bing Maps

① View of East Elevation

Figure 7.6. Case Study 2: Title sheet

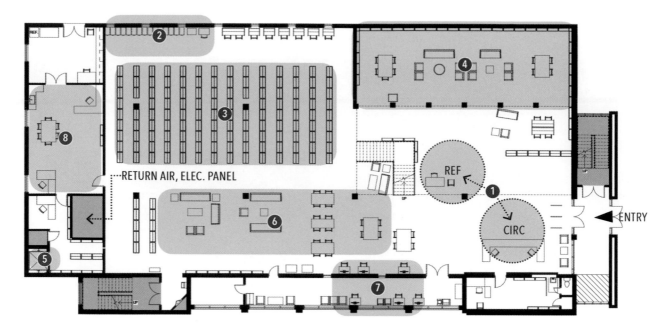

EXISTING MAIN LEVEL

PLAN NOTES

1. The reference and circulation desks are too close together.

2. Microforms are 50 percent empty and seldom used.

3. Per the owner, bound periodicals can be reduced and the general collection can be weeded.

4. The reference area is underutilized.

5. The existing elevator is inaccessible from the public area. Public must access the elevator through the staff workroom and storage area.

6. The existing seating area is inefficient and lacks adequate power receptacles.

7. Computer quantities are insufficient and inefficiently arranged around existing power receptacles.

8. The work room can accommodate additional staff.

Figure 7.7. Case Study 2: Existing main level

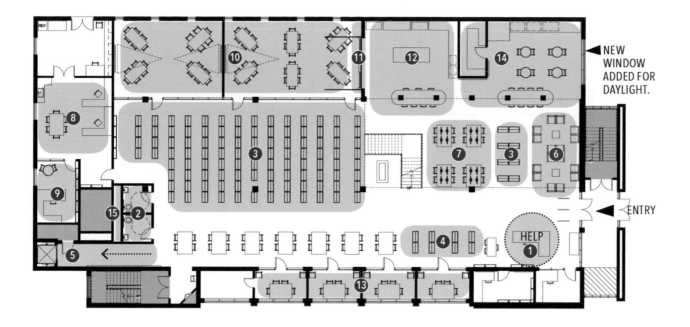

PROPOSED MAIN LEVEL

PLAN NOTES

1. The reference and circulation desks are consolidated to a single help desk.

2. New public toilets are installed and are visible from the help desk.

3. Bound periodicals are eliminated. A portion of the general collection is relocated from the second level to the main level. The overall number of shelves is reduced.

4. The reference collection is reduced and relocated to low 42"-high shelving near the help desk.

5. The elevator is now accessible to the public and is visible from the help desk.

6. New lounge seating is located near the café and entrance.

7. The number of computers is increased; computers are located closer to the help desk.

8. Additional staff space added to existing workroom.

9. New library director's office is created.

10. Two new active learning classrooms are added.

11. Garage door is installed to open the classroom to public area.

12. Copy/print/scanning and project assembly space for students is added.

13. Four new small group study rooms are added.

14. A new café space with storage is added.

15. A new chase is created to maintain access to HVAC return grilles and electrical panels.

Figure 7.8. Case Study 2: Proposed main level

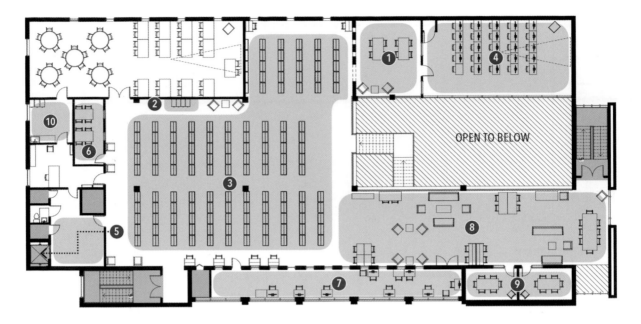

EXISTING UPPER LEVEL

PLAN NOTES

1. Study space at the entry of the instruction room is awkward.

2. Empty card catalog cabinets take up space.

3. General collection can be reduced.

4. Existing library instruction room has outdated traditional computer stations.

5. Existing elevator is inaccessible from the public area. Public must access the elevator through the staff workroom and storage area.

6. Existing small group study room is long and thin, and is furnished with two tables. While this room can accommodate two groups, only one table is used at a time.

7. Computer stations are located on the enclosed porch; the space is long and thin, and does not meet ADA clearance requirements.

8. The existing furniture layout is inefficient and does not provide enough seating and study tables.

9. Two existing small study rooms are heavily utilized and popular with students.

10. Special collections and archival work area is too small and cannot accommodate the storage space necessary for the department. All materials are stored in a damp, dark storage room in the basement.

Figure 7.9. Case Study 2: Existing upper level

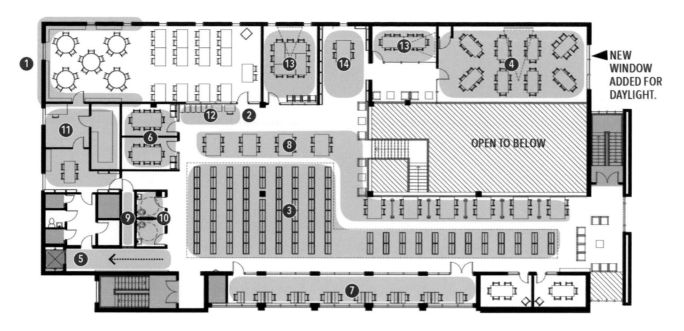

PROPOSED UPPER LEVEL

PLAN NOTES

1. Locked shelving is provided at the perimeter to house and display special collections from the basement.

2. Card catalog cabinets are removed.

3. Number of general collection shelves on this level is reduced.

4. Traditional library instruction room is transformed into a new active learning classroom.

5. The elevator is now accessible to the public.

6. Two small group study rooms are added.

7. Study carrels are located in this space to create a quiet study room. The carrels are an efficient use of space in the long, narrow area.

8. More study tables are added to the second level.

9. A new chase is created to maintain access to HVAC return grilles and electrical panels.

10. New public toilets are installed.

11. Existing storage room and existing small study room are renovated for new special collections and archives space.

12. Microforms are reduced in number and relocated to this corner near special collections and archives.

13. New seminar rooms are added.

14. An alcove is created to house the curriculum collection.

Figure 7.10. Case Study 2: Proposed upper level

PROJECT SUMMARY

MEASURABLES

	EXISTING	NEW	DIFFERENCE	PERCENT
TABLES	13	22	+9	69% INCREASE
SEATS	256	427	+171	67% INCREASE
STUDY ROOMS	5	14	+9	180% INCREASE
COMPUTERS	14	24	+10	71% INCREASE
CARRELS	23	14	-9	39% DECREASE

OWNER'S STATEMENT

" *The Dotti Shelton Learning Commons has been transformational for our campus. The work changed an underutilized facility into the most popular destination on campus for our students, faculty, and staff.* "

–Dr. Barry Buxton
President, Lees-McRae College

PHASING OVERVIEW

The following diagrams illustrated the phasing plans developed for the library. The approach for executing this Road Map was to renovate the library one level at a time, beginning with the main level.

PHASE 1
Phase 1 renovates the library entrance and installs a new consolidated help desk, café, and business center.

PHASE 2
Phase 2 continues with the main level renovations and begins to reconfigure the upper level. The new main level toilets are installed, and a new corridor provides public access to the existing elevator.

PHASE 3
Phase 3 installs new classrooms on the main level.

PHASE 4
Phase 4 renovates and installs a new quiet study area and group study rooms on both levels, and new classrooms, seminar rooms, and curriculum area on the upper level.

PHASE 5
Phase 5 renovates the existing classrooms and installs new group study rooms, quiet room, seminar rooms, and curriculum space.

PHASE 6
Phase 6 renovates the staff, special collections, and archives areas.

Figure 7.11. Case Study 2: Project summary

PHASE 1

A Weed reference collection and clear out the highlighted area.

B Renovate alcove under the existing library instruction room in order to install café, the business center, and the offices at the circulation desk.

C Install new consolidated circulation and reference desk. Add low periodical shelving, lounge seating, and new reference shelving adjacent to the new desk. Relocate computers from existing enclosed porches to new location.

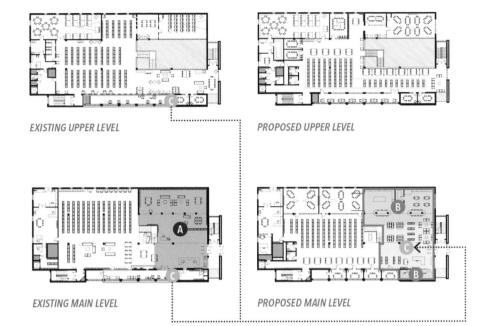

EXISTING UPPER LEVEL   PROPOSED UPPER LEVEL

EXISTING MAIN LEVEL   PROPOSED MAIN LEVEL

PHASE 2

A Weed the collection and reconfigure the shelving layout on the first and second levels.

B Renovate with new finishes and add new toilets.

C Add access to the elevator. Install new finishes in new corridors.

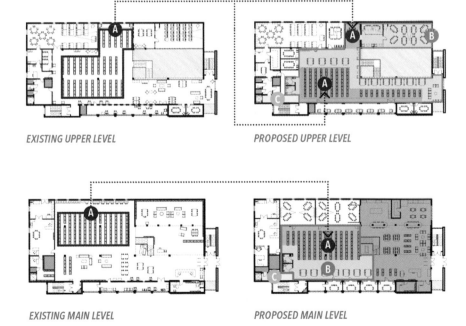

EXISTING UPPER LEVEL   PROPOSED UPPER LEVEL

EXISTING MAIN LEVEL   PROPOSED MAIN LEVEL

NOTE : The shaded gray regions represent areas renovated in previous phases.

Figure 7.12. Case Study 2: Phasing plans

PHASE 3

A Build new classrooms on the main level.

B Relocate the classes that utilize the upper level computer lab to new classrooms on the main level.

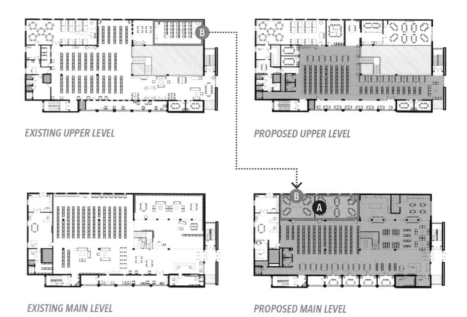

EXISTING UPPER LEVEL

PROPOSED UPPER LEVEL

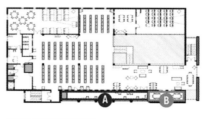

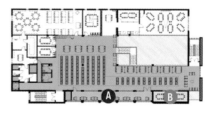

EXISTING MAIN LEVEL

PROPOSED MAIN LEVEL

PHASE 4

A Renovate the identified areas for new group study rooms and quiet room.

B Renovate existing small group study rooms on upper level.

EXISTING UPPER LEVEL

PROPOSED UPPER LEVEL

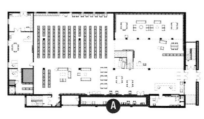

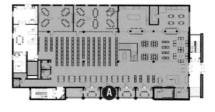

EXISTING MAIN LEVEL

PROPOSED MAIN LEVEL

NOTE : The shaded gray regions represent areas renovated in previous phases.

Figure 7.13. Case Study 2: Phasing plans

PHASE 5

A Renovate existing classroom and add additional small group study rooms, seminar rooms, and curriculum space on upper level.

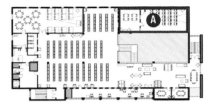

EXISTING UPPER LEVEL

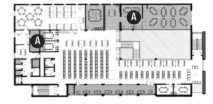

PROPOSED UPPER LEVEL

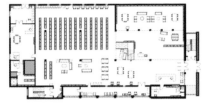

EXISTING MAIN LEVEL

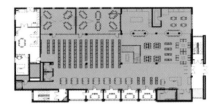

PROPOSED MAIN LEVEL

FROM LOWER LEVEL

PHASE 6

A Renovate staff area.

B Move director into new office.

C Move archives and special collections into new work space from lower level.

D Add lockable special collections shelving along the perimeter of large meeting room. Upgrade finishes in this space as desired.

This completes the library renovations.

EXISTING UPPER LEVEL

PROPOSED UPPER LEVEL

EXISTING MAIN LEVEL

PROPOSED MAIN LEVEL

NOTE : The shaded gray regions represent areas renovated in previous phases.

Figure 7.14. Case Study 2: Phasing plans

CASE STUDY 3

32,000-SQUARE-FOOT ACADEMIC LIBRARY

32,000 SQUARE-FOOT ACADEMIC LIBRARY

PROJECT STATEMENT

This three-story 32,000 SF academic library was built in 1967. A quintessential "modern" campus building erected during the 1960s, it features a concrete structure and was not designed with the necessary infrastructure needed for a modern library. Over the years, minor modifications and upgrades have been made to the existing interior finishes, but the building remained much as originally designed. In 2006, the college erected a remote repository at the rear of the campus to accommodate a print collection that had outgrown the existing library. By relocating seldom used materials to this location, the library was able to create space to meet other needs and to accommodate growth in the staff beyond what was planned for in the 1960s.

PROJECT OBJECTIVES

The primary concerns and objectives to be addressed in the Road Map included the following:

- Consolidate the reference and circulation desks into one staff help desk

- Increase views to the exterior and increase daylight into the center of the main level

- Reduce the footprint of the print reference collection

- Create a learning commons on the main level with an active, inviting atmosphere

- Make the library a collaborative, intuitive, and friendly space for students to hang out

- Eliminate the confusing double-sided entry vestibule

- Create spaces for students and learning center faculty to meet throughout the library

- Add more group study spaces

- Create a larger vending area

Site Plan

Site plan courtesy of Bing Maps

1 Existing Entrance

Existing on-campus repository

- Create a 24/7 study space within the library

- Create a digital media studio/editing lab

- Consolidate the archives collection and related spaces currently dispersed throughout the building

- Relocate the media services department to reduce disruption to library services

Figure 7.15. Case Study 3: Title sheet

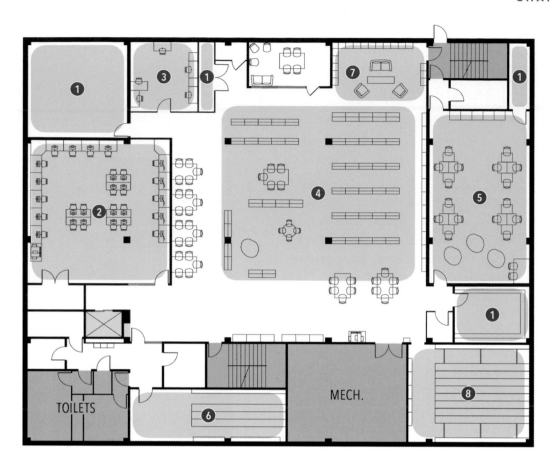

EXISTING LOWER LEVEL ⊕N

PLAN NOTES

1. Archives and special collections areas are fragmented.

2. Computer instruction classroom is inefficiently organized; student desks face the perimeter of the room.

3. Existing video editing room is isolated, hard to find, and far away from the help desk.

4. Education collection is inefficiently organized and occupies much of the lower level.

5. Large, awkwardly sized assembly room is rarely used.

6. This special collections and archives area is too small; the adjacent toilets overflow and flood archive space.

7. Music collection is isolated and rarely used.

8. Back-file periodicals on compact shelving are efficiently organized.

Figure 7.16. Case Study 3: Existing lower level

PROPOSED LOWER LEVEL   ⊕N

PLAN NOTES

1. Archives area is relocated. Assuming that the existing plumbing issues are resolved, the old archive room adjacent to toilets is now used for general library storage.

2. A larger, less used media storage/workroom is relocated to the lower level, with direct elevator access to main level media services area.

3. Education collection is distributed on SF shelving along the perimeter of the floor area; this area is more flexible, with movable furniture.

4. The large assembly room is divided into three seminar rooms.

5. Consolidated special collections and archives area is relocated away from plumbing and toilets.

6. New library instruction room is designed as a flexible, active learning classroom.

7. Collaborative booth seating is added.

Figure 7.17. Case Study 3: Proposed lower level

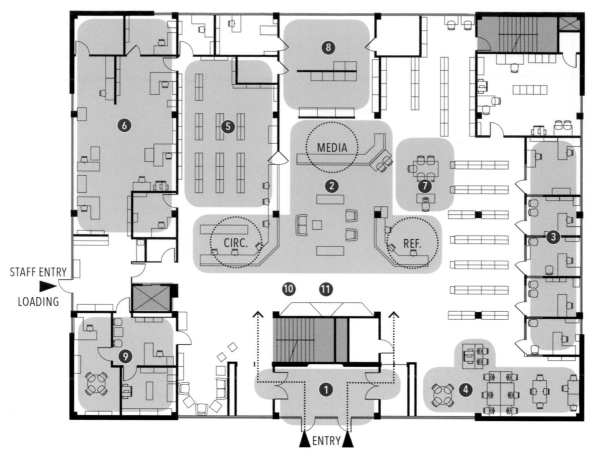

EXISTING MAIN LEVEL ⊕N

PLAN NOTES

1. The entrance is confusing; most people instinctively turn to the right, leading them to the reference desk instead of the circulation desk.

2. Staff desks are too close in proximity, and it is too staff intensive to man both desks.

3. Library staff offices are disconnected from staff work areas.

4. Computer area is too small and congested.

5. Circulation work area is open to the public space.

6. Reference and technical services staff work area is inefficient and uses inappropriate furniture.

7. Reference area is too close to the noisy media desk where how-to equipment demonstrations take place.

8. Media equipment storage area is not secure, and impedes exterior views and daylighting opportunities.

9. Administration area is located adjacent to a high-traffic and noisy loading area and main entrance.

10. Main level does not have public toilet facilities.

11. Interior is dark; all existing windows are blocked by walled spaces.

❝ When we first started the Road Map, the main level had limited seating that was always in use. Students needed access to power for their laptops (and other devices), and wanted more collaborative spaces. Our service model was also shifting–from primarily print-based resources–to electronic materials, and from multiple services desks to consolidated services. The placement of our media services support desk was problematic and disruptive to nearby services. ❞

–Laura Davidson
Dean of Library Information Services at Meredith College

Figure 7.18. Case Study 3: Existing main level

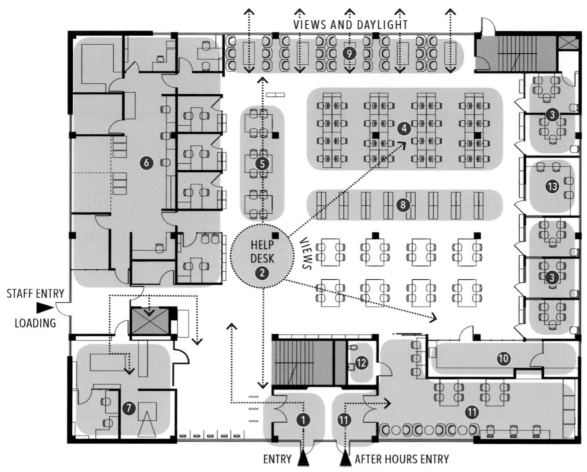

VIEWS AND DAYLIGHT

STAFF ENTRY

LOADING

HELP DESK ②

VIEWS

ENTRY   AFTER HOURS ENTRY

PROPOSED MAIN LEVEL   ⊕ N

PLAN NOTES

1. Lobby has a single entry point when the library is open.

2. Help desk is consolidated to a single location.

3. Staff offices are converted to group study rooms.

4. Computer area is expanded and reconfigured.

5. Study tables for library consults and study are located near the help desk.

6. Consolidated work area is adjacent to help desk; new circulation work area is enclosed and separate from the public area.

7. New media service area for equipment storage is enclosed for demonstration and minimal disruption to others. This room is located near the elevator for easy equipment transport between levels.

8. Minimal reference collection on 42" DF shelving is used to separate computers from reading tables.

9. Lounge seating is provided near windows for views and serves as a waiting area for computers.

10. Project assembly space includes an enclosed print/copy/scan center to contain noise from copiers and other equipment.

11. Twenty-four-hour study space is accessible from the lobby through double doors; study space lobby doors are locked when library is open, and when the library is closed the after-hours entry doors unlock to allow access to the space from the lobby.

12. Unisex toilet is provided for twenty-four-hour study space.

13. Staff office is converted into new digital media studio.

Figure 7.19. Case Study 3: Proposed main level

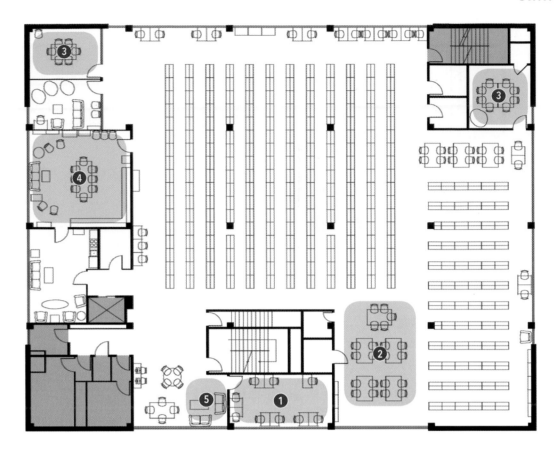

EXISTING UPPER LEVEL ⊕N

PLAN NOTES

1. Carrels are inefficiently organized in a small room.

2. Tables are randomly organized.

3. Group study room introduces too much noise to a "quiet" level when in use; staff constantly receive noise complaints.

4. Special collections reading room is underutilized.

5. Lounge furniture promotes socializing and noise.

Figure 7.20. Case Study 3: Existing upper level

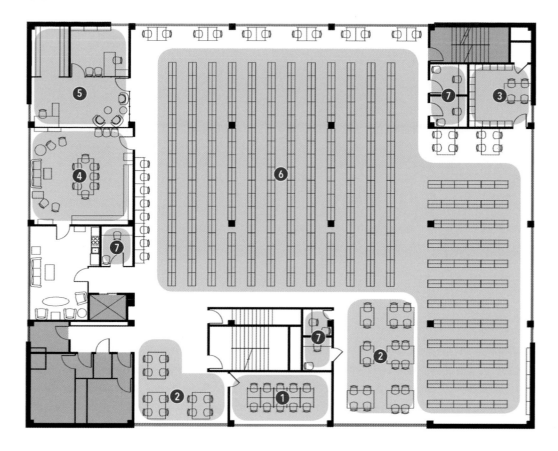

PROPOSED UPPER LEVEL ⊕N

PLAN NOTES

1. Silent study room is created that includes reconfigured carrels.

2. Study tables are reorganized.

3. Former noisy small group study room houses seldom used music collection and becomes another quiet study space.

4. Special collections reading room will double as administration conference room when not in use.

5. Administration area is relocated to quiet level, introducing adult supervision to upper level.

6. Existing stack arrangement remains the same.

7. Five individual study rooms are created for focused silent study.

GENERAL COMMENTS

- The upper level is designated as quiet level; all lounge furniture and group study rooms are eliminated to promote quiet study.

Figure 7.21. Case Study 3: Proposed upper level

PROJECT SUMMARY

MEASURABLES

	EXISTING	NEW	DIFFERENCE	PERCENT
TABLES	34	66	+32	94% INCREASE
SEATS	265	388	+123	46% INCREASE
STUDY ROOMS	3	10	+7	233% INCREASE
COMPUTERS	36	66	+30	83% INCREASE
CARRELS	35	32	-2	6% DECREASE

OWNER'S STATEMENT

" *The Master Plan created for us has been endlessly useful, even if much of it is unrealized. As library leaders have retired and new department heads hired, the plans have given context for talking about a vision for the building and a footprint for their units. I am pleased with how well the plan has held up through these leadership transitions. I thought the process for creating the plan was excellent. It left my staff and college leadership with great confidence in the results.* "

–Laura Davidson
Dean of Library Information Services, Meredith College

Figure 7.22. Case Study 3: Project summary

PHASING OVERVIEW

The following pages illustrate the entire phasing plan developed for the library. It is fairly straightforward; it does not involve any relocation, weeding, or shifting of the general collection. The most involved piece of the total renovation is the main level. This level must remain open during the renovation, with the exception of a possible short-term closure during a summer break. It was important to the college that the initial phases involve the main level so that donors would immediately see progress and improvement to critical student spaces.

Below is a summary of the six phases required to implement the Road Map.

PHASE 1

Phase 1 vacates the western half of the main level so it can be renovated. In order to accomplish this, functions currently in that area must be displaced, but remain operational. Some functions will be relocated to temporary spaces, and others will be moved to their permanent locations. Once this area is cleared out, a temporary barrier will be erected to divide the operational side of the main level from the side being renovated. With a renovation of this magnitude, noise is always a concern, so the contractor will have to coordinate his activities with the academic calendar to minimize disruptions, such as finals week, etc.

PHASE 2

Phase 2 clears out and renovates the balance of the main level to create the learning commons. This completes the main level renovations.

PHASE 3

Phase 3 temporarily relocates several lower level spaces, and renovates approximately a third of that level. This creates a new, expanded place for the archives department and a new collaborative instruction classroom for the computer instruction room.

PHASE 4

Phase 4 renovates the existing computer instruction room into the new media storage/workroom and office suite; renovates the existing archives area and converts into the new video editing office and general library storage room.

PHASE 5

Phase 5 renovates the balance of the lower level.

PHASE 6

To complete the renovation, phase 6 renovates the balance of the upper level, and involves upgrading finishes and furniture.

Figure 7.23. Case Study 3: Phasing overview

PHASE 1

(A) Renovate the upper level group study rooms to receive new administration offices.

(B) Relocate administration staff to new offices on upper level.

(C) Temporarily relocate technical services to the large assembly room on lower level.

(D) Consolidate the circulation desk functions with existing reference desk.

(E) Temporarily relocate the copy room functions to upper level study room.

(F) Temporarily relocate circulation work area to empty copy room.

(G) Renovate the west side of main level.

Figure 7.24. Case Study 3: Phasing plans

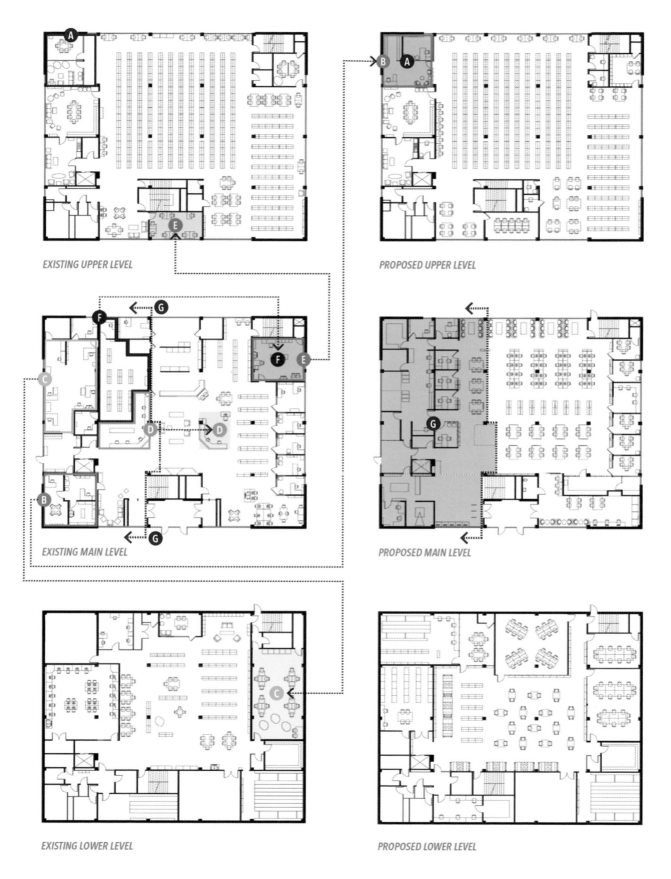

EXISTING UPPER LEVEL

PROPOSED UPPER LEVEL

EXISTING MAIN LEVEL

PROPOSED MAIN LEVEL

EXISTING LOWER LEVEL

PROPOSED LOWER LEVEL

Figure 7.25. Case Study 3: Phasing plans

PHASE 2

(A) Relocate media services desk to new location completed in phase 1.

(B) Temporarily relocate media services work area, storage, and offices to lower level storage area.

(C) Relocate combined circulation and reference desk to new location completed in phase 1.

(D) Relocate reference offices to new location completed in phase 1.

(E) Relocate circulation work area to new location completed in phase 1.

(F) Relocate technical services area to new location completed in phase 1.

(G) Temporarily relocate balance of reference area resources and seating to lower level open area.

(H) Temporarily relocate main level computers to lower level large assembly room.

(I) Renovate eastern half of main level.

After the main level renovation is completed, temporarily relocated spaces designated for the eastern half of the main level should move back to their final locations:

(J) Move copy room functions (temporarily relocated to upper level in step E of phase 1) to final location on main level.

(K) Move computers (temporarily relocated to lower level in step H of phase 2) to final location on main level.

(L) Move reference area (temporarily relocated to lower level in step G in phase 2) to final location on main level.

This completes the main level renovation.

NOTE :
The shaded gray regions represent areas renovated in previous phases.

Figure 7.26. Case Study 3: Phasing plans

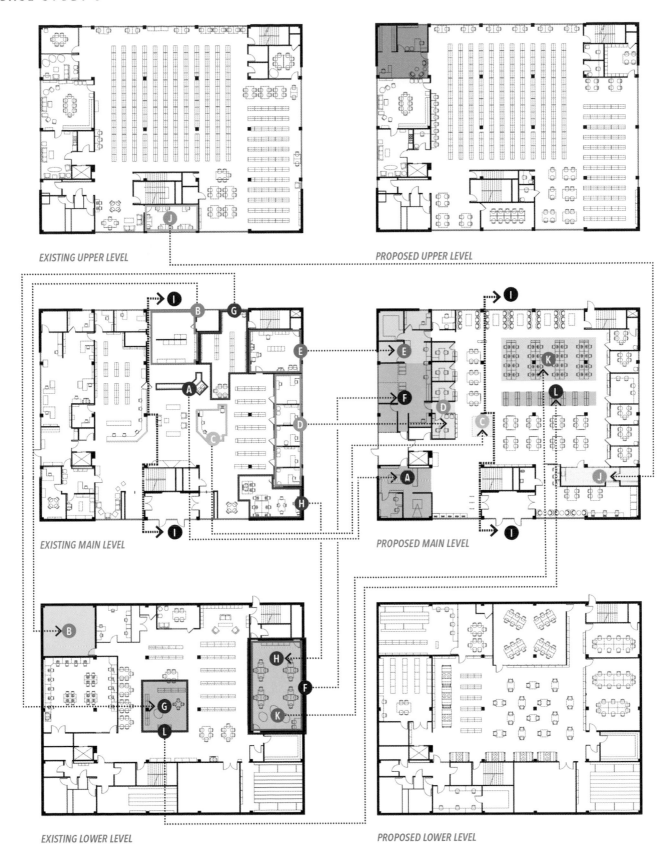

Figure 7.27. Case Study 3: Phasing plans

PHASE 3

A Move music scores from lower level to new location on upper level.

B Temporarily relocate video editing room to upper level study room.

C Temporarily relocate items in media storage room to large assembly room.

D Renovate identified lower level area.

After the renovation of the identified area in the lower level in step D is completed:

E Move computer instruction classroom to final location.

F Move existing archive storage to final location.

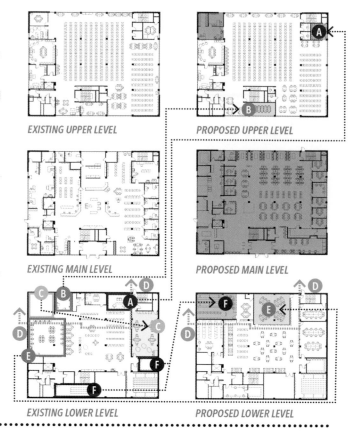

EXISTING UPPER LEVEL   PROPOSED UPPER LEVEL

EXISTING MAIN LEVEL   PROPOSED MAIN LEVEL

EXISTING LOWER LEVEL   PROPOSED LOWER LEVEL

PHASE 4

A Renovate former computer instruction classroom and archive storage room vacated in phase 3.

B Relocate media equipment storage to final location.

C Relocate video editing room (temporarily relocated to upper level in step B in phase 3) to final location.

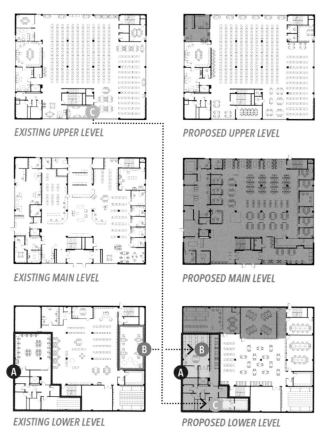

EXISTING UPPER LEVEL   PROPOSED UPPER LEVEL

EXISTING MAIN LEVEL   PROPOSED MAIN LEVEL

NOTE :
The shaded gray regions represent areas renovated in previous phases.

EXISTING LOWER LEVEL   PROPOSED LOWER LEVEL

Figure 7.28. Case Study 3: Phasing plans

PHASE 5

(A) Renovate balance of lower level.

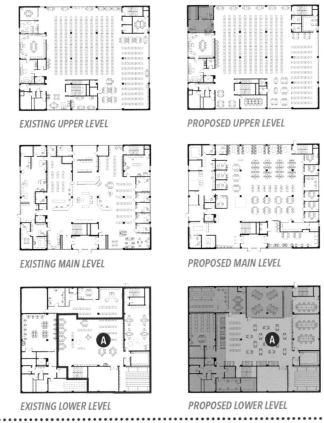

EXISTING UPPER LEVEL

PROPOSED UPPER LEVEL

EXISTING MAIN LEVEL

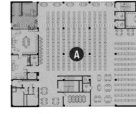

PROPOSED MAIN LEVEL

EXISTING LOWER LEVEL

PROPOSED LOWER LEVEL

PHASE 6

(A) Renovate balance of upper level to complete the overall library renovation.

EXISTING UPPER LEVEL

PROPOSED UPPER LEVEL

EXISTING MAIN LEVEL

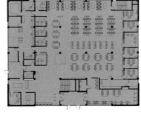

PROPOSED MAIN LEVEL

NOTE :

The shaded gray regions represent areas renovated in previous phases.

EXISTING LOWER LEVEL

PROPOSED LOWER LEVEL

Figure 7.29. Case Study 3: Phasing plans

CASE STUDY 4

40,000-SQUARE-FOOT PUBLIC LIBRARY

40,000 SQUARE-FOOT PUBLIC LIBRARY

PROJECT STATEMENT

This 40,000 SF single-story public library was originally constructed in 1975, and was expanded and renovated in 2003. The library was designed as a regional library headquarters that served and supported the library systems of several counties. Located on Gloucester Street, the library featured a large central corridor with the library on one side and the regional library offices on the other side. In 2012, however, the county library board voted to form a single county library system and no longer needed to be a regional headquarters for the surrounding counties, leaving the existing regional offices unnecessary. Furthermore, after nearly forty years of service, the library had become tired and struggled to accommodate current technologies and meet current user needs.

PROJECT OBJECTIVES

The primary concerns and objectives to be addressed in the Road Map included the following:

- Improve the entry sequence from Gloucester Street

- Eliminate the large angled corridor

- Improve lines of visibility from staff help desk locations

- Provide a children's area able to accommodate large groups of children for story hour and special programs

- Consolidate staff and improve efficiency

- Increase computers and available technology

- Create new public restrooms in lieu of existing single-occupant toilet rooms

- Create a larger meeting room for community events

- Add small group study rooms

- Reduce footprint of print collection to reflect reduction of reference and periodical resources

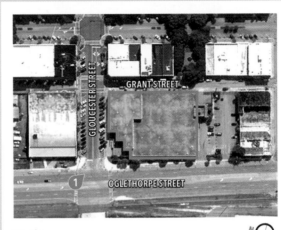

Site Plan

Site plan courtesy of Bing Maps

1 View of North Elevation

Figure 7.30. Case Study 4: Title sheet

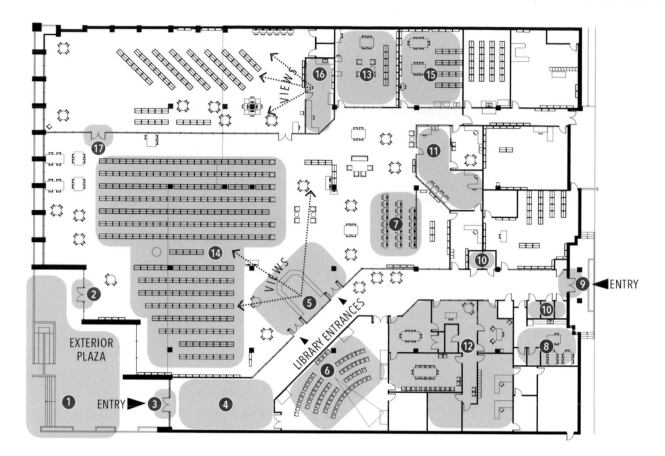

EXISTING MAIN LEVEL

N⊕

PLAN NOTES

1. Existing ramp and plaza planters block views into the library; plaza is underutilized.

2. Emergency exit is locked from outside; this is confusing to those entering the building.

3. Public entrance from main street is recessed and hard to find.

4. Corridor that formerly separated the library from regional offices is inefficient.

5. Staff cannot see entrance from help desk.

6. Public meeting room is oddly shaped and too small.

7. Computer area is too small and heavily utilized by library patrons.

8. Staff break room is adequate.

9. Existing elevated planters block views to the entrance of the library from the parking lot.

10. Five unisex toilet rooms create a security oversight issue for staff.

11. Staff work room is undersized.

12. Former regional library offices are underutilized.

13. Young adult room is adequate.

14. Long ranges of adult fiction and nonfiction shelving are half empty; aisles are too long for browsing.

15. Local history room is too small.

16. Views of the children's room are impeded by shelving.

17. Entrance to the children's area allows adult users to enter unseen by children's area staff.

Figure 7.31. Case Study 4: Existing main level

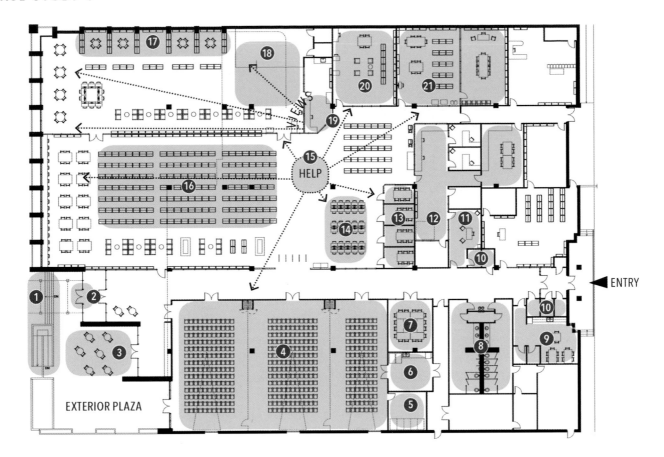

PROPOSED MAIN LEVEL

N ⊕

PLAN NOTES

1. New stairs align with new main street-level library entrance; plaza walls are removed to improve visibility.

2. New street-level entry is on axis with internal corridor.

3. New café seating activates the exterior plaza.

4. New community meeting room provides seating for more than four hundred and can be divided into three separate rooms.

5. Furniture storage is provided for the meeting room.

6. Kitchenette space is provided for the meeting room.

7. New seminar room is added.

8. New public toilets are provided.

9. Existing staff break room remains the same.

10. Existing unisex toilet rooms to remain as family facilities.

11. Librarian director office with private toilet.

12. Staff work room is reorganized and expanded.

13. Four new small group study rooms are added.

14. Computer area includes additional public computers.

15. Centralized help desk offers better viewing capability.

16. Adult fiction and nonfiction collections are consolidated and reorganized.

17. Children's collection is reorganized with low shelving and integrated seating.

18. Story hour area overflows into larger children's area.

19. Children's help desk offers views to the children's area.

20. Young adult room remains unchanged.

21. Local history space is enlarged.

Figure 7.32. Case Study 4: Proposed main level

PROJECT SUMMARY

MEASURABLES

	EXISTING	NEW	DIFFERENCE	PERCENT	
TABLES	29	30	+1	3%	INCREASE
SEATS	266	689	+423	159%	INCREASE
STUDY ROOMS	0	4	+4	400%	INCREASE
COMPUTERS	32	40	+8	25%	INCREASE
AUDITORIUM SEATS	64	406	+342	534%	INCREASE

OWNER'S STATEMENT

" *The Road Map provided us a 'how-to' guide on breaking down the facility master plan into manageable bite size chunks. Thanks to the Road Map, we were able to get grant funding from the state and a local match from the Glynn County Board of Commissioners to renovate the children's room, teen room, and part of the local history room at the Brunswick Library. Also, since the plan gave us a minimal cost way to renovate the St. Simons Library, the state and Glynn County Board of Commissioners provided funding to completely finish that project.*

The facility master plan and the Road Map gave the libraries the ammunition to get the ball rolling on the project. Thanks to this design, we qualified for a capital outlay grant from the state to help pay for the remainder of the cost. "

–Geri Lynn Mullis
Director, Marshes of Glynn Libraries

PHASING OVERVIEW

In order to implement the Road Map for the library and simultaneously allow the library to remain in operation throughout the process, the work is organized into phases and steps that can accommodate a gradual transformation of the existing space as necessary. The Road Map phases are generally organized to make internal shifts to prepare for renovations to first renovate the library side of the building, including the meeting rooms and bathrooms. Finally, the renovation is completed with upgrading of the non-library side of the building.

PHASE 1
Phase 1 includes the renovation of the children's area and the main public area of the library.

PHASE 2
Phase 2 clears out the southeast corner of the library so the spaces on the west side of the library can be vacated and renovated.

PHASE 3
Phase 3 renovates the workroom and entrance corridor.

PHASE 4
Phase 4 renovates the balance of the building.

PHASE 5
Phase 5 completes the project by relocating the remaining temporary areas to their final locations.

Figure 7.33. Case Study 4: Project summary

PHASE 1

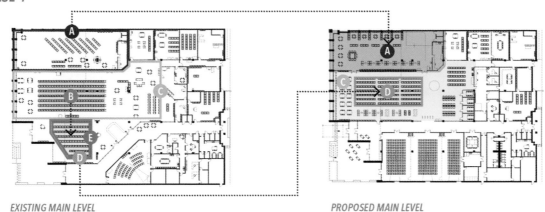

EXISTING MAIN LEVEL   PROPOSED MAIN LEVEL

Ⓐ Renovate the children's room; excess space in this area allows it to be renovated without displacing any furniture.

Ⓑ Reduce the size of the print collection; temporarily shift books onto adjacent shelving.

Ⓒ Renovate the main public area.

Ⓓ Relocate temporarily shelved print collections to new 66" shelving in main public area.

Ⓔ Remove remaining empty shelving used to temporarily store print collection.

PHASE 2

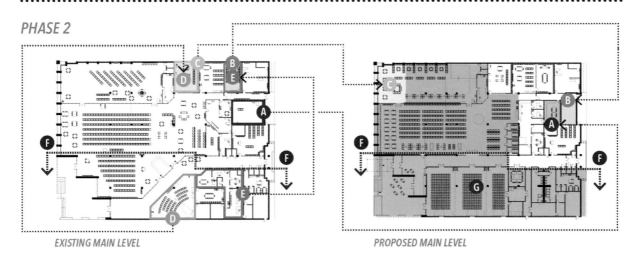

EXISTING MAIN LEVEL   PROPOSED MAIN LEVEL

Ⓐ Consolidate friends of the library storage and renovate storage room.

Ⓑ Organize and move contents of storage room into newly renovated storage room.

Ⓒ Temporarily relocate young adult area into highlighted zone of children's area.

Ⓓ Temporarily hold meeting room functions in the existing young adult room.

Ⓔ Temporarily relocate offices to cleared out storage room.

Ⓕ Create temporary limits of construction.

Ⓖ Renovate west side of the temporary limits of construction, including exterior plaza work.

NOTE : The shaded gray regions represent areas renovated in previous phases.

Figure 7.34. Case Study 4: Phasing plans

PHASE 3

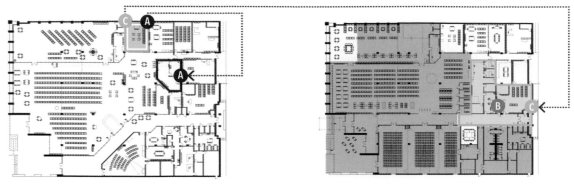

EXISTING MAIN LEVEL   *PROPOSED MAIN LEVEL*

Ⓐ Temporarily relocate existing workroom to existing young adult room.

Ⓑ Renovate workroom and adjacent entrance, including rest of the entrance corridor.

Ⓒ Move temporarily relocated workroom to new and final workroom location.

PHASE 4

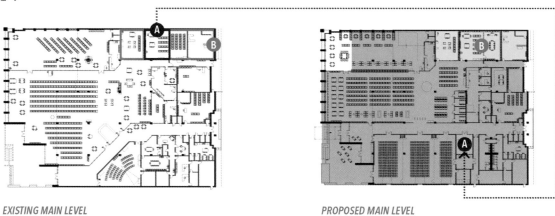

EXISTING MAIN LEVEL   *PROPOSED MAIN LEVEL*

Ⓐ Temporarily relocate local history room to new conference room.

Ⓑ Renovate the balance of the library.

NOTE : The shaded gray regions represent areas renovated in previous phases.

Figure 7.35. Case Study 4: Phasing plans

PHASE 5

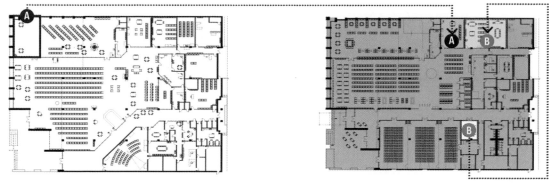

EXISTING MAIN LEVEL   PROPOSED MAIN LEVEL

Ⓐ Move young adult area (temporarily relocated to the children's area in step C of phase 2) to its final location.

Ⓑ Move local history room (temporarily relocated to conference rooms in step A of phase 4) to its final location.

NOTE : The shaded gray regions represent areas renovated in previous phases.

Figure 7.36. Case Study 4: Phasing plans

CASE STUDY 5

180,000-SQUARE-FOOT ACADEMIC LIBRARY

180,000 SQUARE-FOOT ACADEMIC LIBRARY

PROJECT STATEMENT

This university's library was built in 1966 and is located in the center of campus. It is a six-story structure with two underground levels, ground elevation at the third level, and entry to the library from an elevated pedestrian bridge on the fourth level. During its first forty years the library had few internal and organizational changes, with the exception of adding new student computers. Over the years, however, the university doubled in population and the library was falling short of meeting student and faculty needs and failing to keep up with technological changes.

In 2012, the library embarked on a Road Map that focused on improving and maximizing the potential of its existing facility and identified a phased implementation approach that would allow for small incremental improvements as funds became available. This successful approach has allowed for several small renovations to take place instead of doing nothing while waiting for money to be raised.

The Road Map identified the following goals to address:

- Provide more student seating with adequate power and data

- Provide more student group collaborative space

- Consolidate staff departments and service points

- Increase technology presence throughout the library

- Expand food service to accommodate longer and more diverse student usage patterns

- Provide active learning classrooms, visualization labs, and presentation and media editing studios

- Identify departments that can be relocated to the off-site repository, where ample space and parking are available

Site Plan

Site plan courtesy of Bing Maps

Aerial view of library, 1966

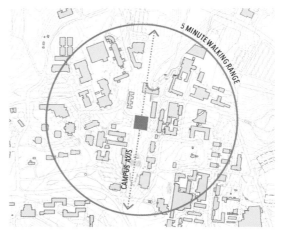

Walking distance from library

Figure 7.37. Case Study 5: Title sheet

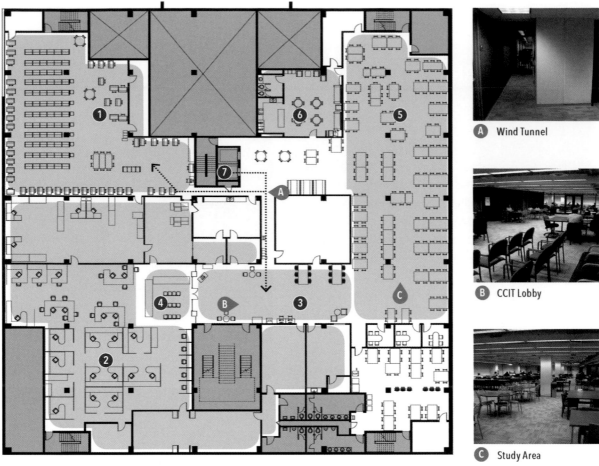

A Wind Tunnel

B CCIT Lobby

C Study Area

EXISTING SECOND LEVEL   ⊕
N

PLAN NOTES

1. The existing narrow passage, known as the "wind tunnel," leads to the level's only return air grilles, creating a noisy and "windy" area and posing a security risk due to minimum visibility.

2. University CCIT (Clemson Computing and Information Technology) department drives heavy traffic to this floor.

3. Existing lobby is extremely undersized; students waiting for CCIT department service create crowded conditions at the beginning of the semester.

4. Service counters in CCIT workroom are disruptive to the work space and are generally too small to accommodate student lines.

5. Formerly stack space, this area has become a randomly organized study area composed of donated furniture from previous dining hall renovations, and lacks adequate power and data.

6. The staff lounge for the entire library has no access to daylight, and is not adjacent to any staff space.

7. There is no signage directing users from the main elevators to the lobby.

Figure 7.38. Case Study 5: Existing second level

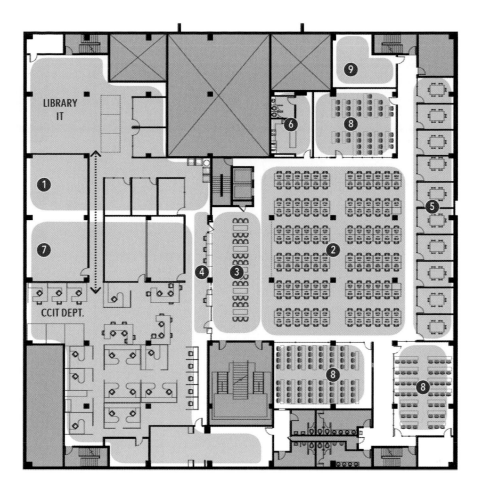

PROPOSED SECOND LEVEL ⊕ N

PLAN NOTES

1. Library IT department is relocated adjacent to CCIT and is now closer to consolidated library computer commons and technology-equipped small-group collaboration spaces.

2. Computers are consolidated from five different locations to this area. This area also serves as overflow seating during high traffic occasions at CCIT.

3. Reoriented and expanded lobby receives people directly from the elevator and stairs, providing immediate visibility to CCIT and library IT service counters/windows.

4. Service counters/windows are reconfigured to allow lines to form in the lobby instead of department workroom.

5. Ten new technology-equipped small-group collaboration spaces are created.

6. Overall staff lounge is reduced to serve as break room for second level staff.

7. CCIT department remains; staff workstations are reconfigured to add additional spaces.

8. Three library instruction rooms located on this level can be used as additional general computers when classes are in session.

9. Additional storage for library IT is created.

Figure 7.39. Case Study 5: Proposed second level

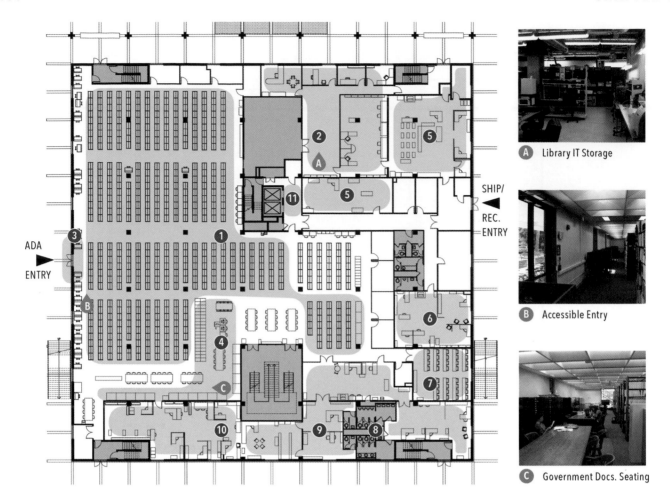

A Library IT Storage

SHIP/
REC.
ENTRY

B Accessible Entry

C Government Docs. Seating

ADA
ENTRY

EXISTING THIRD LEVEL

N

PLAN NOTES

1. Staff estimates government documents can be reduced by 50 percent and the remainder moved to off-site repository.

2. Library IT moves to the second level since it currently blocks valuable windows and views to the exterior.

3. Existing accessible entrance with no staff supervision.

4. Maps and microforms to be relocated off-site.

5. Binding and acquisitions to be relocated off-site.

6. Acquisitions receiving to be relocated off-site.

7. Existing library instruction room is too small and is oriented incorrectly with the front of the room at the entrance.

8. Public toilets are landlocked.

9. Vacant area formerly occupied by the academic success center serves as flex space. When occupied by non-public departments, it blocks access to the public toilets, forcing students to use the toilets on another level.

10. Docs/tech processing to be relocated to off-site offices.

11. Current elevators are shared by staff and the public. On this level, the public exits elevators into the staff area. Ideally, staff would have a designated elevator in this space that is not accessible to the public.

Figure 7.40. Case Study 5: Existing third level

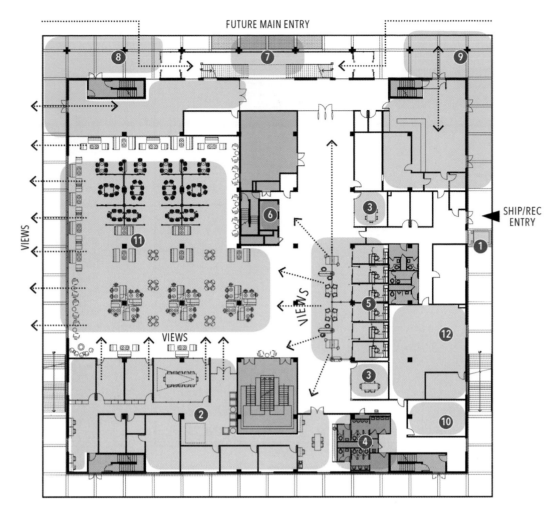

PROPOSED THIRD LEVEL

⊕
N

PLAN NOTES

1. New staff elevator connects fourth level staff work space to this level.

2. Library administration department is relocated from the fourth level to consolidate the administrative team and to free highly desirable space on the fourth level for the public. This new location also offers some visual supervision of the third level commons.

3. Small-group collaboration spaces are added adjacent to librarian offices for team consults.

4. Previously landlocked public toilets are made accessible.

5. Reference librarian offices allow visual supervision of third level entrance and internal circulation.

6. Centralized elevators are open to everyone, with more space and better views of the entire level.

7. New main entrance receives visitors from the east and west and directs them to the third and fourth levels.

8. New coffee shop allows access to outdoor seating.

9. New café with access to outdoor seating.

10. Office space is designated for faculty senate.

11. Expanded storefront in new commons space increases visibility to and from library commons.

12. Facilities department is located near shipping and receiving.

Figure 7.41. Case Study 5: Proposed third level

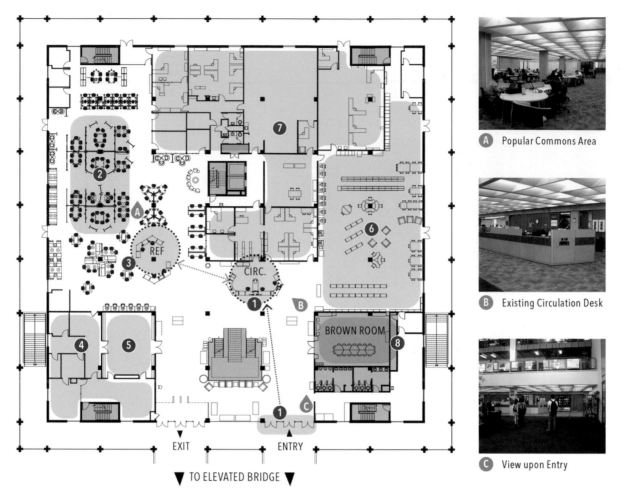

A Popular Commons Area

B Existing Circulation Desk

C View upon Entry

EXISTING FOURTH LEVEL

PLAN NOTES

1. Entrance from elevated bridge has limited views, but the circulation/help desk is immediately identifiable.

2. The commons area represents the library's most recent move toward a collaborative, flexible, and interactive space. This area is popular with students.

3. The reference desk is too close to the circulation desk.

4. The current administration area is undersized and isolated from other administrative personnel and staff members.

5. The Byrnes Room, currently a museum display area, could be converted to serve as a collaborative study or seminar space.

6. The shelving and collections in this area have already been removed and relocated. The current space is underutilized and ready for renovation.

7. The central hard-walled staff spaces are underutilized due to the recent staffing shifts. The location of the elevators requires students and food service deliveries to be made through surrounding staff areas.

8. The Brown Room, currently a display area, could be converted to serve as a collaborative study or seminar space.

Figure 7.42. Case Study 5: Existing fourth level

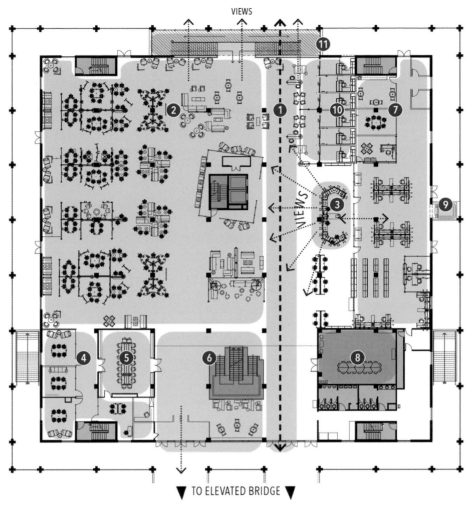

VIEWS

▼ TO ELEVATED BRIDGE ▼

PROPOSED FOURTH LEVEL ⊕ N

PLAN NOTES

1. Upon entering the library, views extend through the entire level.

2. Student commons is expanded.

3. The centralized and consolidated help desk has supervisory views to the library's entrances and vertical circulation.

4. The former administrative area becomes "hoteling" space serving those who need temporary space.

5. The Byrnes Room is updated to serve as a small conference room.

6. Library exit remains in this location with expanded security.

7. A centralized work space is created for reference, circulation, and ILL staff with flexible furniture.

8. Space renovated as an isolated step in the Road Map (see the Edgar Brown Digital Resources Laboratory case study later in this chapter for more details).

9. A new staff-only elevator connects the third and fourth levels exclusively.

10. The reference librarian offices are accessible to the public, in close proximity to the help desk, and adjacent study tables allow for impromptu meetings and consults.

11. New stairs connect the fourth level to the new main entrance to the south created on the third level.

Figure 7.43. Case Study 5: Proposed fourth level

PROJECT SUMMARY

MEASURABLES

	EXISTING	NEW	DIFFERENCE	PERCENT
TABLES	198	139	-59	30% DECREASE
SEATS	1,575	2,360	+785	50% INCREASE
STUDY ROOM	24	40	+16	67% INCREASE
COMPUTERS	199	297	+98	49% INCREASE
CARREL	309	529	+220	71% INCREASE

OWNER'S STATEMENT

" *The Road Map helps us maintain our focus on the library as a learning lab and meeting place for Clemson students, reinforcing our desire to be relevant in the life of the university. With Road Map in hand, I am able to respond quickly to opportunities and feel confident that each decision made is part of a larger plan. By using the Road Map study, Cooper Library will continue down the road to reach our destination.* "

–Kay Wall
Dean of Libraries (Retired), Clemson University

PHASING OVERVIEW

The following pages illustrate the phasing plans developed for the library. In order to implement the Road Map and simultaneously allow the library to remain in operation throughout the process, the work is organized into phases and steps that allow for a gradual transformation of the existing space into the new proposed plan by renovating the library one level at a time, beginning with the second level.

Below is a summary of the three phases required to implement the Road Map.

PHASE 1
Phase 1 renovates the second level.

PHASE 2
Phase 2 renovates the third level.

PHASE 3
Phase 3 renovates the fourth level.

Figure 7.44. Case Study 5: Project summary

PHASE 1

A Relocate the oversized collection in this area to the off-site repository.

B Renovate the former oversized collection area to receive library's IT department.

C Renovate and rearrange furniture in university's IT department (CCIT).

D Upon completion of both the university's and library's IT areas, relocate library IT department to their final location.

E Renovate denoted areas to make new computer instruction rooms.

F Renovate balance of floor to receive seating and small group study rooms.

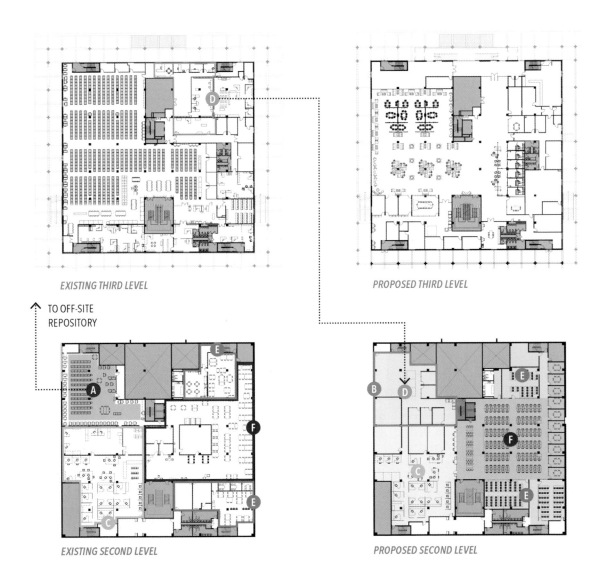

EXISTING THIRD LEVEL

PROPOSED THIRD LEVEL

TO OFF-SITE REPOSITORY

EXISTING SECOND LEVEL

PROPOSED SECOND LEVEL

Figure 7.45. Case Study 5: Phasing plans

PHASE 2

A Relocate staff to new locations at the off-site repository.

B Relocate gov docs to off-site repository.

At this point, the entire third level has been vacated and could be renovated as one project, or individual areas could be renovated separately as smaller projects, if needed, and in any order.

C Renovate administration area.

D Relocate administration staff on fourth level to final location.

E Renovate library facilities department and faculty senate space.

F Relocate library facilities department and faculty senate space to final locations.

G Renovate areas to receive new food service providers.

H Renovate the balance of the floor to receive new finishes, furniture, power, etc.

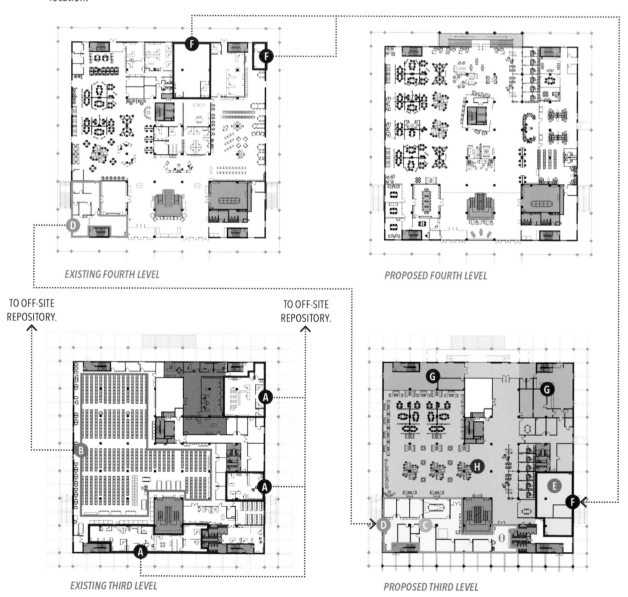

EXISTING FOURTH LEVEL   *PROPOSED FOURTH LEVEL*

TO OFF-SITE REPOSITORY.   TO OFF-SITE REPOSITORY.

EXISTING THIRD LEVEL   *PROPOSED THIRD LEVEL*

Figure 7.46. Case Study 5: Phasing plans

PHASE 3

Ⓐ Renovate this area for new collaboration and hoteling spaces.

Ⓑ Relocate staff to their new locations at the off-site repository.

Ⓒ Renovate this area to receive new circulation, reference, and ILL work areas.

Ⓓ Move circulation, reference, and ILL staff from their current locations to their final locations.

Ⓔ Renovate the balance of the floor.

NOTE: The second and third levels are not affected in the fourth level phasing strategy because these levels were completed in the second and third level phasing plans.

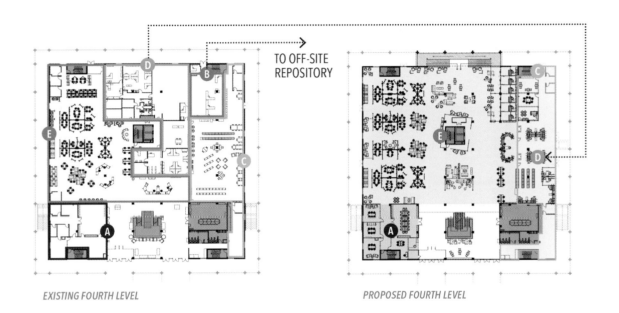

EXISTING FOURTH LEVEL   *PROPOSED FOURTH LEVEL*

Figure 7.47. Case Study 5: Phasing plans

ROAD MAP

In 2008, the library participated in the development of a traditional master plan that recommended consolidating off-site collections back to campus and expanding the existing library with two underground two-story additions with an estimated cost of more than $70 million. This plan was presented to the university administration in October of 2008, a week before the economic downturn, rendering it impractical and putting it on hold indefinitely. Unfortunately, the library's needs and inadequacies remained unaddressed.

In the two years that followed, the library abandoned the notion of bringing its remotely stored items back to the main library and instead built a new, larger off-site repository with a high-bay storage strategy to free up more space within the existing library.

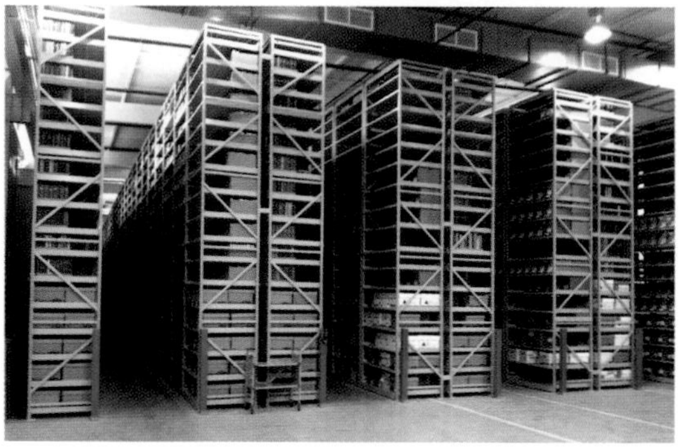

Off-site repository with high-bay storage

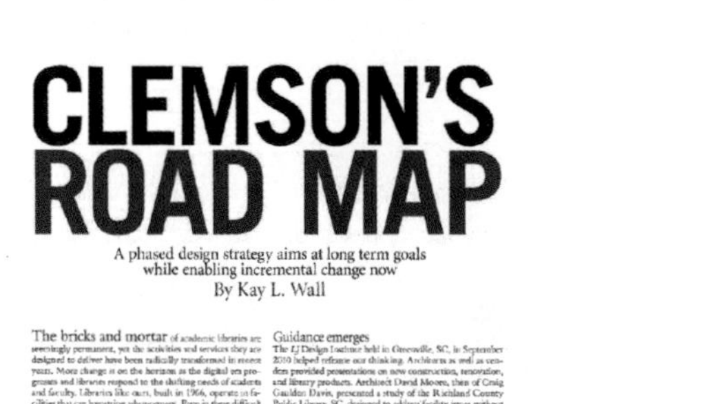

CLEMSON'S ROAD MAP

A phased design strategy aims at long term goals while enabling incremental change now

By Kay L. Wall

November 2011 *Library Journal* article

During those two years, the library also experienced significant changes. These changes were implemented in a piecemeal approach and led to the realization that a Road Map that offered a framework to inform future decisions was necessary. Some of the changes that precipitated the need for a Road Map included the following:

- Consolidation of service points and staff areas over time
- Change to a selective federal depository rather than a shared regional model, allowing for the selective review of documents on the third level for retention
- Installation in 2009 of compact shelving on the lowest level to reduce the footprint of the general collection
- Development of a partnership between the library and university IT customer support that relocated the CCIT (Clemson Campus Information Technology) department onto the second level of the library
- Creation of a fourth level commons area in 2010
- Creation of a new and improved off-site repository
- Planning of the recently vacated Academic Success Center space on the third level

In 2010, Dean Wall first applied the term *Road Map* to differentiate this work from that of a traditional master plan, primarily due to the inherent flexibility that the phasing diagrams and incremental implementation opportunities provided. In November of 2011, Wall authored an article in *Library Journal* and this new approach received national attention through this publication and subsequent conference presentations all over the country.

Figure 7.48. Case Study 5: Road Map

EDGAR BROWN DIGITAL RESOURCES LABORATORY

The Brown Room was originally designed to be a museum space (image B). As demand for more technology, digital resources, and teaching spaces increased, this room was identified as one to be converted into a highly visible high-tech collaborative classroom (image A). The project was completed as an independent renovation, as mentioned in the Road Map.

Forty-two years after the Edgar Brown Room's inaugural dedication in 1971, the university partnered with Dell and the National Science Foundation to develop and implement a first-of-its-kind multidisciplinary, multipurpose meeting space featuring the very latest technologies in high performance computing, remote collaboration, and information visualization for students and researchers from all academic disciplines. The Digital Resources Laboratory (DRL) was a bold first step for Clemson University in creating new learning spaces on campus where all members of the campus community are invited to both learn about advanced computing technologies as well as use those technologies to enhance teaching and research.

At the time of publication, the room features:

- A large visualization wall comprising fifteen 46" HD displays

- A sixteen-node computational cluster for simulation, data processing, and computation, and five-node dedicated visualization cluster for image processing and rendering

- A very high-bandwidth network connection to the campus network and high-speed Internet outside the university

- Laptops for sixteen students with software customization available

- Network and video connections in the floor that allow students to share their work

- An HD videoconferencing system

- Side-by-side projectors for dual-input projection onto a large refinished wall space

- Reconfigurable and removable furniture

Image A

Image B

Figure 7.49. Case Study 5: Edgar Brown Digital Resources Laboratory

R.M. COOPER LIBRARY ADOBE DIGITAL STUDIO

Clemson University developed a new learning and research studio space within the R.M. Cooper Library with the goal of facilitating student and faculty digital literacies in the context of courses, research, and creative inquiry. This studio, which highlights the partnership between Clemson University and Adobe, is a space where students and faculty can invent new learning opportunities and transform communication practices across disciplines while showcasing the use of Adobe products in the twenty-first-century workplace.

Working with state-of-the-art publishing software and hardware, Adobe-trained experts lead workshops, consult one-on-one with students and faculty on a wide range of projects, and assist in the production of high-quality work for distribution to the university and the public. The Adobe Digital Studio features audio and video recording studios and provides printing equipment to produce high-quality publications, including variable data and display posters. The Adobe Digital Studio also gives users access to the latest and best technologies to create high-quality print and digital media, and is outfitted with workstation furniture designed to encourage mobility and collaboration.

The studio houses computer hardware and peripherals (including tablets and devices), workstations in multiple operating systems, monitors, wall-mounted displays, printers, scanners, audio-video equipment and projection technologies, and, of course, Creative Cloud software.

Figure 7.50. Case Study 5: Adobe Digital Studio

Image A - Before

Image B - After

Image C - Before

Image D - After

Image E - Before

Image F - After

By opening the solid wall of the lobby (image A), more visibility is given to the Adobe Digital Studio (image B)—which is located on the fifth level, one level above the entrance to the library—thus connecting it with the surrounding library space and increasing the sense of transparency.

Prior to the renovation, this space housed 90" DF back-file periodical shelving and seating (images C and E). The Road Map identified this as more common space similar to what had already been installed on the fourth level. Identifying and accommodating the location of this new studio after the Road Map was published demonstrates the Road Map's inherent flexibility in allowing incremental renovations to take place without nullifying the entire plan.

Figure 7.51. Case Study 5: Adobe Digital Studio

CASE STUDY 6

300,000-SQUARE-FOOT ACADEMIC LIBRARY

300,000 SQUARE-FOOT ACADEMIC LIBRARY

PROJECT STATEMENT

The 300,000 SF academic library is located in the heart of the campus and in the center of a historic 1926 Italian Renaissance–detailed quadrangle. It was originally constructed in 1956 as a two-story building with a basement, with the upper two levels added in the 1980s. Today the library's location is regarded as less than ideal, and while serious consideration has been given to removing it and constructing a new library elsewhere, the university felt it important to evaluate the current building's potential in the event that it should remain. In addition to developing a detailed Road Map, the university also engaged in a study of what could be done aesthetically to the exterior envelope to make it more attractive, to relate more to the surrounding historic context, and to improve the building's overall energy performance.

PROJECT OBJECTIVES

The primary concerns and objectives to be addressed in the Road Map include the following:

- Reduce the footprint of the general collection and government documents

- Install new waterproofing in the basement and replace deteriorating compact shelving

- Add computer teaching lab with seating for 250+

- Incorporate and consolidate the university's Center for Academic Success (CAS) and Student Support Services (SSS) into the library

- Build an off-site institutional repository elsewhere on campus

- Add small-group collaborative spaces, seminar rooms, presentation rooms, and active learning classrooms

- Create a new faculty Lounge

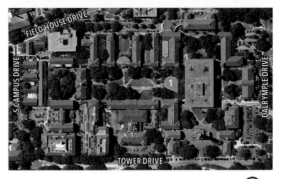

Site Plan

⊕N

Site plan courtesy of Bing Maps

① Original 1956 Library

- Create a new, separate graduate student lounge and study space

- Create a digital media studio and resource center

- Create specialized technology spaces, visualization studios, and a 24/7 study area for students

- Address faculty and staff space deficiencies

Figure 7.52. Case Study 6: Title sheet

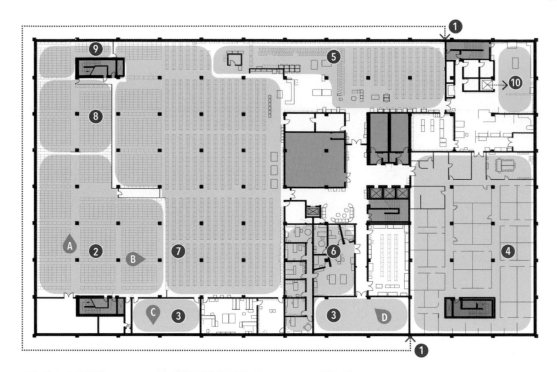

A Old Compact Shelving **B** Rotted Subflooring **C** General Storage **D** General Storage

EXISTING BASEMENT LEVEL

PLAN NOTES

1. Existing below-grade wall needs to be waterproofed to stop moisture infiltration prior to any work being done on this level.

2. General collection compact shelving is old and inoperable, with rotting subfloor in some places, and needs to be replaced.

3. Existing rooms are empty or are used for miscellaneous storage.

4. Collection development, collection management, and cataloging workstations are extremely oversized and inefficient.

5. Microfilm and microform area occupies a large footprint and is rarely utilized.

6. Digital services offices are too small and shoehorned into the former music library space.

7. Government documents are housed primarily on traditional shelving and occupy a large footprint.

8. The special collections overflow, housed on compact shelving from the special collections library, is not properly conditioned.

9. Active water leak prevents this corner from being utilized as storage.

10. Shipping and receiving from the level above is located adjacent to the elevator.

Figure 7.53. Case Study 6: Existing basement level

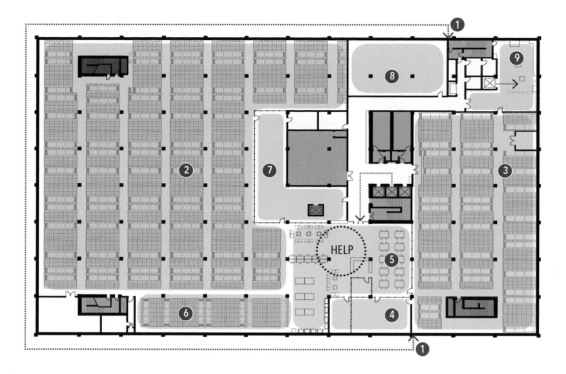

PROPOSED BASEMENT LEVEL

PLAN NOTES

1. Install waterproofing to eliminate water infiltration issues and repair leak in corner.

2. New compact shelving is installed to house majority of the general collection in approximately 2,650 DF units.

3. Government documents are consolidated into new compact shelving in a closed controlled stack arrangement.

4. Government documents workroom is located with direct access to government documents and visual oversight of the reading room.

5. Government documents and general reading room are located near the existing vertical circulation core.

6. Microfilm and microforms are consolidated into new compact shelving and located near general help desk.

7. Circulation and ILL workroom are located at a central location adjacent to the majority of the general collection.

8. Dedicated library general storage room is created near shipping and receiving area.

9. Area remains a shipping and receiving area for this level.

Figure 7.54. Case Study 6: Proposed basement level

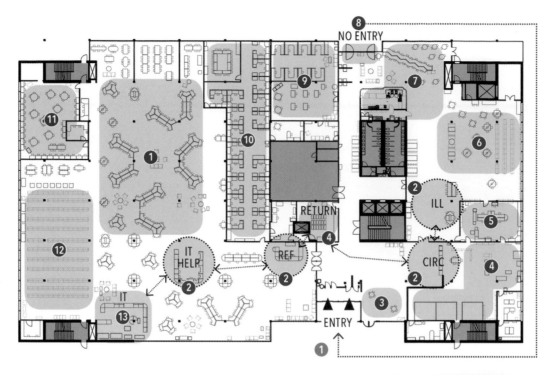

EXISTING MAIN LEVEL

PLAN NOTES

1 Existing South Elevation

1. Computer commons is inefficient and haphazard in its arrangement, but is popular with students.

2. There are too many service points; these should be consolidated.

3. Inefficient lobby space is sometimes used for art displays.

4. Circulation desk and workroom are too far away from the entry, not near the book return area.

5. ILL workspace is defined by open cubicles and is not secure, private, or visible from the entrance.

6. Periodical area is inefficient and underutilized.

7. Café space is too small, not enclosed, and not visible from the main entrance; noise typically spills over to the periodical and ILL area.

8. Entry doors are locked from the exterior; users must go around outside of the building to the main entrance on the opposite side.

9. Faculty technology center near the café is problematic and is often mistaken for student space.

10. Research and instructional services workroom is close to the reference desk, but is not accessible to faculty and students, and lacks appropriate consult space.

11. Recently renovated tutoring space is highly used but is too small.

12. Reference collection previously weeded and vacated; empty 90" DF shelving blocks views to exterior.

13. IT printing services and work area is open to the public and is inefficient, noisy, unsightly, and unsecured.

Figure 7.55. Case Study 6: Existing main level

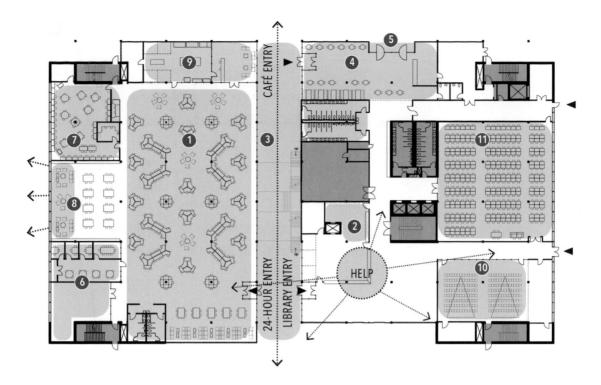

PROPOSED MAIN LEVEL

PLAN NOTES

1. Computer commons space is rearranged to be more efficient and provide more study and computing space. Due to the fact that this space is now utilized 24/7, toilets are added to this area.

2. All service points have been combined into one help desk with an adjacent work area.

3. Breezeway connects exterior quads. Users no longer have to walk around the building to enter the library.

4. A larger café is provided with exterior breezeway access, and has direct connection to the loading dock. The overhead gate allows for separation between café and library space when closed.

5. Entry doors are now open into the café area.

6. Outpost CAS (Center for Academic Services) and SSS (Student Support Services) provided here. More space is provided on upper levels.

7. Tutoring space remains as is. Additional tutoring outpost space is provided on other levels.

8. Views are open to the exterior.

9. IT services are consolidated, enclosed to reduce noise, and private in order to secure after hours.

10. 200+ seat multipurpose room is provided for library special events and lectures.

11. 250+ seat computer lab and teaching space is provided for general university testing and computing needs.

Figure 7.56. Case Study 6: Proposed main level

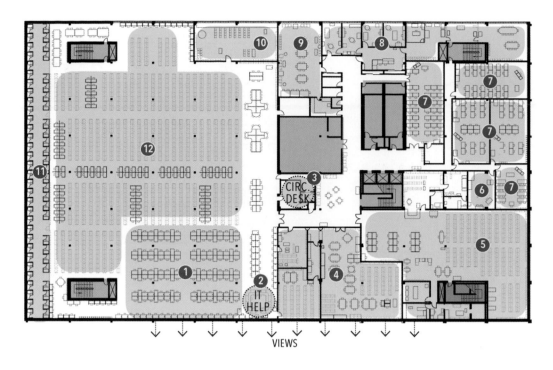

VIEWS

EXISTING SECOND LEVEL

PLAN NOTES

1. Computer lab is underutilized. The university intends to remove these desktop computers.

2. IT help desk has no workroom, is open to the public, and is visually cluttered.

3. All levels with general collection have a circulation desk that requires staff.

4. Education department is undersized, subdivided, and landlocked. This space has tremendous views to the exterior.

5. Music department is self contained, requires a separate help desk, and is landlocked. Oral history is also located in this space.

6. IT server room is not near IT staff.

7. Existing four classrooms are long, narrow, not conducive for A/V use, and not as flexible as active learning spaces. The access corridor is too narrow for the number of students using these rooms.

8. Administration suite is not cohesive and lacks sufficient offices; visitors must go through workspace to access the administration conference room.

9. Staff break room and kitchen are antiquated and not inviting.

10. Multipurpose room is long and narrow with built-in counters that limit room layout possibilities.

11. Graduate student carrels have low walls and no sound control, and do not have adequate power.

12. General collection and carrels are randomly organized; carrels do not have adequate power.

Figure 7.57. Case Study 6: Existing second level

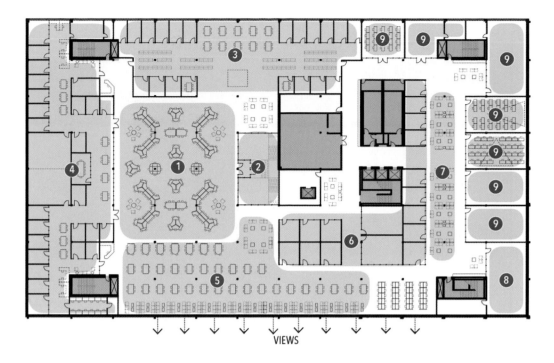

VIEWS

PROPOSED SECOND LEVEL ⊕

PLAN NOTES

1. Centrally located information commons is provided with collaborative computer spaces.

2. Entry from monumental stairs allows students to enter directly into the information commons from breezeway below.

3. Research and instructional services department is located at the top of the monumental stair. Reference offices are accessible to students, and large enough for faculty to consult with students. Reference collection is reduced and housed on low 42" DF shelving units.

4. New consolidated 9,500 SF CAS and SSS spaces frees 6,588 SF elsewhere on campus, and these student services complement the adjacent research and instructional services department.

5. Reconfigured general reading room with study tables and soft lounge seating along exterior walls takes advantage of beautiful views to the quad.

6. New collaborative group study rooms and presentation rooms are provided to meet student demand.

7. Soft lounge seating provides collaboration space, study space, and a place for students and faculty to congregate prior to and after classes.

8. New visualization room provides a specialized classroom for the incorporation of digital content and simulated environments.

9. Seven new active learning classrooms feature flexible seating.

Figure 7.58. Case Study 6: Proposed second level

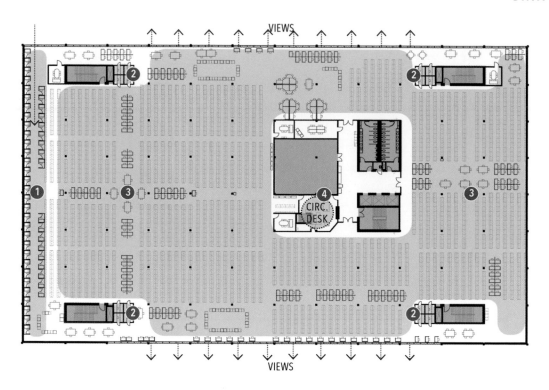

EXISTING THIRD LEVEL

PLAN NOTES

1. Graduate student carrels have low walls, no sound control, and inadequate power.

2. Four individual study rooms are located at each stair.

3. General collection and carrels are randomly organized. Carrels are in high-traffic areas, and do not have adequate power.

4. All levels with general collection have a circulation help desk that requires staff.

Figure 7.59. Case Study 6: Existing third level

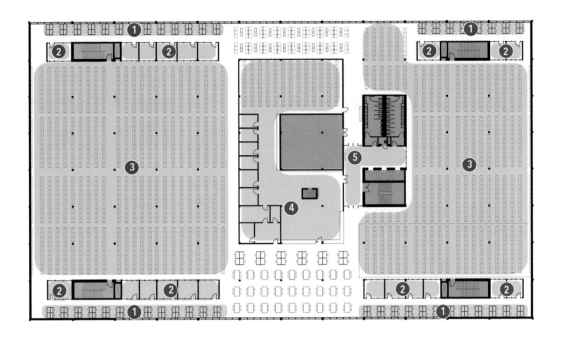

PROPOSED THIRD LEVEL

PLAN NOTES

1. Study carrels are located in quiet spaces along the perimeter.

2. Collaborative group study rooms are provided with glass walls for visual transparency.

3. A portion of the general collection is consolidated to this level. Study carrels are removed from between stacks and additional shelving is provided to increase the shelving capacity on this level.

4. Music education and oral history workrooms and circulation help desk are consolidated in this area. The music education collection becomes a mediated stack. Related open-stack materials for both music and education are nearby within the general collection stacks, allowing for the flexible adjustment of those collections in the future.

5. Theft detection is installed on this level and in the basement. Circulating materials can now be checked out at each level, thus eliminating the need for theft detection at all library entrances on the main level.

Figure 7.60. Case Study 6: Proposed third level

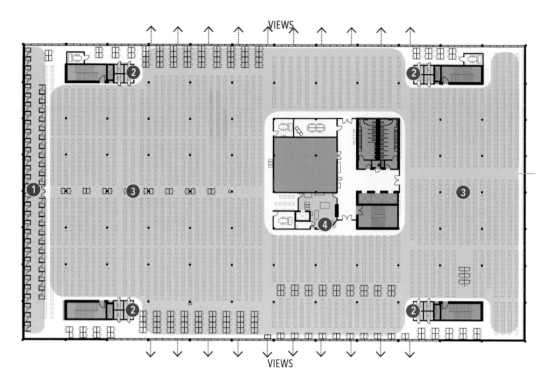

EXISTING FOURTH LEVEL

PLAN NOTES

1. Graduate student carrels have low walls, no sound control, and inadequate power.

2. Four individual study rooms are located at each stair.

3. General collection and carrels are randomly organized; carrels are in high-traffic areas and do not have adequate power.

4. All levels with general collection have a circulation help desk that requires staff.

Figure 7.61. Case Study 6: Existing fourth level

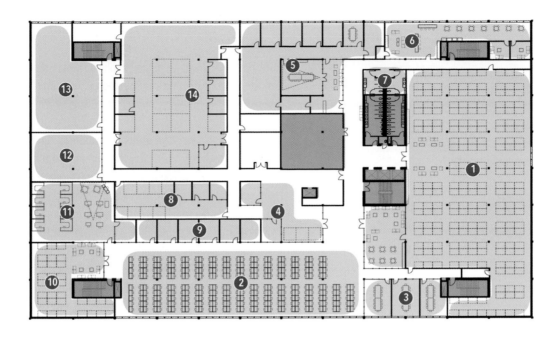

PROPOSED FOURTH LEVEL

PLAN NOTES

1. Graduate student carrels are consolidated to graduate suite with access to the graduate lounge and lockers.

2. Study carrels are added to this level to provide a quiet/silent study area.

3. Three seminar rooms are provided primarily for graduate student and faculty use.

4. New administration services suite is provided and serves as the public entry for staff areas.

5. New administration suite is provided adjacent to majority of staff space.

6. Staff lounge is located on this level, adjacent to a majority of staff offices, and has views to the exterior.

7. New staff toilets are added to accommodate the increased number of staff members on this level.

8. Digital services department is relocated from the lower level.

9. New quiet group study/project rooms are provided for faculty and graduate students.

10. New faculty suite is adjacent to the relocated faculty tech center.

11. Faculty tech center is located in close proximity to the IT staff.

12. Institutional repository is located in close proximity to IT staff and cataloging work area.

13. IT offices, workroom, and storage are located adjacent to other staff areas for increased technological collaboration.

14. Collection development, collection management, and cataloging work area has adequately sized workstations and is located in close proximity to other staff departments.

Figure 7.62. Case Study 6: Proposed fourth level

EXISTING FACILITY OVERVIEW

EXISTING FOURTH LEVEL

EXISTING THIRD LEVEL

EXISTING SECOND LEVEL

EXISTING FIRST LEVEL

EXISTING BASEMENT LEVEL

SUMMARY

The floor plan diagrams to the left illustrate that more than half of the library's existing configuration is dedicated to storing books.

In addition to the government documents and reference collection shelving, there are approximately 6,000 DF units in the library for the general collection. Per discussions with the university library staff, it is reasonable to assume that this collection can be weeded by 10 percent, reducing the general collection by 600 DF units. As part of this Road Map, an off-site repository will be built elsewhere on campus property with an initial capacity to house 1,000 DF units of the general collection. This scenario requires that a minimum of 4,400 DF units remain in the library to house the general collection.

BREAKDOWN

6,000	General collection DF units
– 600	10 percent of collection is weeded
– 1,000	DF units moved to off-site repository
4,400	Minimum number of general collection DF units to remain

KEY

Existing Shelving

DF   Double-Faced Shelving

Figure 7.63. Case Study 6: Existing facility overview

PROPOSED FACILITY OVERVIEW

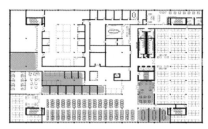

PROPOSED FOURTH LEVEL

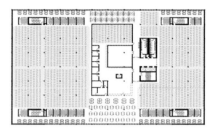

PROPOSED THIRD LEVEL

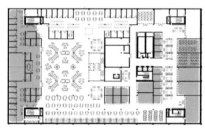

PROPOSED SECOND LEVEL

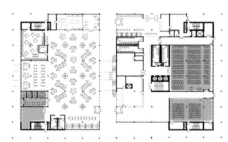

PROPOSED FIRST LEVEL

PROPOSED BASEMENT LEVEL

SUMMARY

The general collection footprint is reduced from more than 50 percent of the library to approximately two levels. The majority of the general collection is housed in new compact shelving on the basement level and on existing metal shelving on the third level. This creates space for:

- 34,000 SF of new student support and program spaces to be added to the library

- 15,683 SF of space in the core campus surrounding buildings to be freed up by relocating CAS, SSS, and nearby computer labs into the library

New student support and program spaces* include:

- Computer lab with seating for 250+

- Multipurpose room with seating for 200+

- Eleven additional classroom/seminar/presentation rooms

- Thirty two additional group study rooms

- Digital services and institutional repository spaces

- Graduate student lounge

- CAS (Center for Academic Support) and SSS (Student Support Services).

  *This does not include all the realized net increases to individual departments or seating throughout the library. Net increases to seating and other components are summarized in the programming summary table that follows.

KEY

⬤ Reconfigured collection

⬤ New student support and program spaces

Figure 7.64. Case Study 6: Proposed facility overview

PROJECT SUMMARY

MEASURABLES

	EXISTING	NEW	DIFFERENCE	PERCENT
CLASSROOMS	6	17	+11	183% INCREASE
SEATS	1,959	3,447	+1,488	76% INCREASE
STUDY ROOM	11	42	+31	282% INCREASE
COMPUTERS	249	417	+168	67% INCREASE
CARREL	743	856	+113	15% INCREASE

OWNER'S STATEMENT

"*Middleton Library is a modern three-story library built in the fifties that was expanded to five stories in the eighties. It totals 325,000 SF in area and is located in the center of LSU's historic quad. The library's modern style conflicts with the surrounding Italian Renaissance architecture and has always been a building that did not suit its surroundings.*

Through the years, several interior spaces underwent renovation without a unified objective, so in 2014, the university developed a Road Map to set the direction for future renovations and determine which LSU departments and functions should be located in an updated twenty-first-century century library. We wanted a plan to transform Middleton into a library that our students expect so that when limited funds became available, portions of the plan could be implemented.

This Road Map provided valuable information that helped inform long term decisions regarding the library. Due to the library's age (fifty-plus years), deferred maintenance issues, its objectionable location, future campus growth patterns, and understanding the cost and time required to fully implement the Road Map, the university decided to prioritize the library's phasing to focus on main level improvements only. In the meantime, the university would evaluate the feasibility of constructing a new library in a different location."

–Mary K. Miles
Associate Director, Planning/Space Management/Interior Design, Louisiana State University

Figure 7.65. Case Study 6: Project summary

REPOSITORY ANALYSIS

SUMMARY

As a part of revisions to the Road Map, and at the request of the university, an analysis was provided to assess the physical requirements needed to house approximately 6,500 DF shelving units of materials comprised of the following collections:

1,200,000 ±	General Collection Volumes
50,000 ±	Music Collection Volumes
175	DF Units of Microforms
1,000	DF Units of Government Documents

The following options were studied and sized accordingly. The size of the repository in each option varied depending on the storage method used.

Option A
30,200 SF

Option A is a 30,200 SF repository utilizing the 35'-tall high-bay storage system.

Option B
54,000 SF

Option B is a 54,000 SF repository utilizing 12'-tall compact shelving.

Option C
114,000 SF

Option C is a 114,000 SF repository that reuses existing 90" metal shelving units taken from the existing library.

CONCLUSION

Each of the options was analyzed to provide a comparable cost analysis to determine the optimum, most cost-effective solution. Factors considered include the size and cost of the building, and the cost of each corresponding shelving system (including labor and moving costs to reuse the existing shelving in option A).

Figure 7.66. Case Study 6: Repository analysis

PHASING OVERVIEW

The following pages illustrate the phasing plans developed for the library. In order to implement the Road Map and simultaneously allow the library to remain in operation throughout the process, the work is organized into phases and steps that allow for a gradual transformation of the existing space into the new proposed plan by renovating the library one level at a time, beginning with the basement level.

Below is a summary of the six phases required to implement the Road Map.

PHASE 1
Phase 1 begins with the construction of an off-site repository. Waterproofing is installed where needed in the basement, and new compact shelving is installed that will be used to consolidate the general collection from the upper levels. Finally, staff and services are moved from the basement and it is renovated.

PHASE 2
In phase 2 the general collection continues to be weeded and the fourth level is renovated.

PHASE 3
Weeding of the general collection is continued in phase 3. The third level is cleared out and renovated.

PHASE 4
Phase 4 renovates a portion of the second level.

PHASE 5
Phase 5 renovates the first level and the balance of the second level.

PHASE 1
Before commencing phase 1, an off-site repository must be built.

- **(A)** Manage the general collection materials to remain in the basement, to be removed, or to be relocated to the repository.
- **(B)** Temporarily move microfilm and microforms to area formerly designated for reference materials on the main level.
- **(C)** Discard existing carrels in the highlighted area and weed/shift the collection as necessary. Temporarily relocate staff from basement to designated areas on the second level. Build temporary walls as needed.
- **(D)** Renovate designated area and install new compact shelving while shifting the remaining general collection.
- **(E)** Relocate government documents to new compact shelving.
- **(F)** Renovate balance of basement and install new compact shelving to receive general collection materials from upper levels in subsequent phases.
- **(G)** Move microfilm and microforms (temporarily located to the main level in step B of phase 1) to final location.
- **(H)** Move ILL to new location.

Figure 7.67. Case Study 6: Phasing plans

EXISTING FOURTH LEVEL

PROPOSED FOURTH LEVEL

EXISTING THIRD LEVEL

PROPOSED THIRD LEVEL

EXISTING SECOND LEVEL

PROPOSED SECOND LEVEL

EXISTING FIRST LEVEL

PROPOSED FIRST LEVEL

TO REPOSITORY
OR REMOVE

EXISTING BASEMENT LEVEL

PROPOSED BASEMENT LEVEL

Figure 7.68. Case Study 6: Phasing plans

PHASE 2

Ⓐ Manage the print materials on the fourth level to determine what can be removed or relocated to the repository. Move the remaining items to the new compact shelving on the basement level.

Ⓑ Temporarily store carrels in the new general storage room created in phase 1.

Ⓒ Renovate the fourth level in its entirety.

Ⓓ Move administration to their new and final location.

Ⓔ Move staff (temporarily located on the second level in step C of phase 1) to their final location.

Ⓕ Move IT staff to their final location.

Ⓖ Move faculty technology center to its final location.

Ⓗ Move carrels on second and third levels to fourth level quiet study area and graduate student suite.

Ⓘ Move carrels from their temporary location on the basement level to fourth level quiet study area and graduate student suite.

NOTE :

The gray shaded regions represent areas renovated in previous phases.

Figure 7.69. Case Study 6: Phasing plans

Figure 7.70. Case Study 6: Phasing plans

PHASE 3

(A) With carrels removed and relocated to the fourth level in phase 2, in-fill and configure shelving to reflect proposed layout. Manage and adjust the collection accordingly to determine what can be relocated to the basement level, be removed, or be relocated to the repository, and what should remain on the third level.

(B) Renovate core area to receive music, education, and oral history departments and small circulation offices.

(C) Construct small group study rooms and renovate the fourth level in its entirety.

(D) Move music, education, and oral history departments to their final locations.

(E) Move part of circulation department to its final location.

NOTE :

The gray shaded regions represent areas renovated in previous phases.

Figure 7.71. Case Study 6: Phasing plans

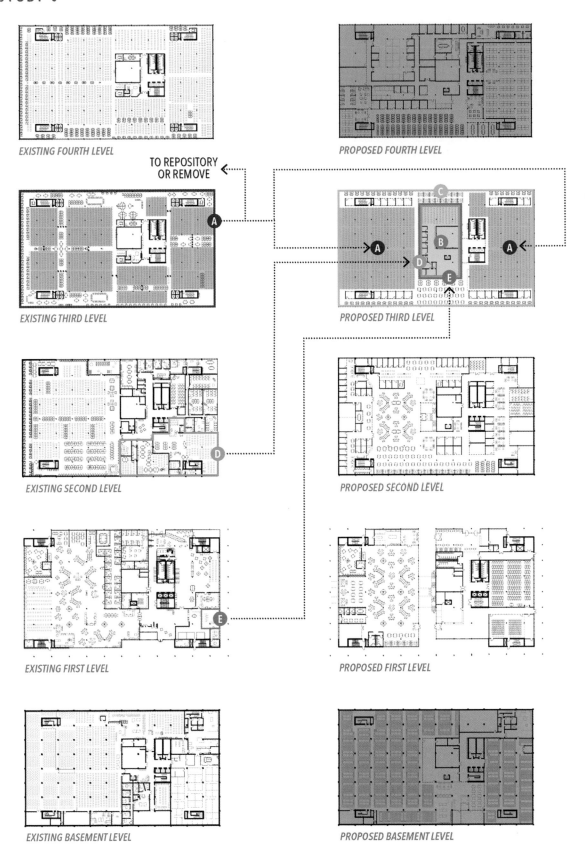

EXISTING FOURTH LEVEL

PROPOSED FOURTH LEVEL

TO REPOSITORY
OR REMOVE

EXISTING THIRD LEVEL

PROPOSED THIRD LEVEL

EXISTING SECOND LEVEL

PROPOSED SECOND LEVEL

EXISTING FIRST LEVEL

PROPOSED FIRST LEVEL

EXISTING BASEMENT LEVEL

PROPOSED BASEMENT LEVEL

Figure 7.72. Case Study 6: Phasing plans

PHASE 4

A With carrels removed and relocated to the fourth level in phase 2, manage and adjust the collection accordingly to determine what can be relocated to the basement or third level, be removed, or be relocated to the repository.

B Take five existing classrooms off-line; fourth level seminar rooms may be used in the meantime.

C Renovate second level in its entirety.

D Move research and instruction department to its final location.

E Center for Academic Services (CAS) and Student Support Services (SSS) relocate from elsewhere on campus to their new and final location in the library.

F Move tutoring, ITS, and the computer commons to a temporary location on the second level.

NOTE :

The gray shaded regions represent areas renovated in previous phases.

Figure 7.73. Case Study 6: Phasing plans

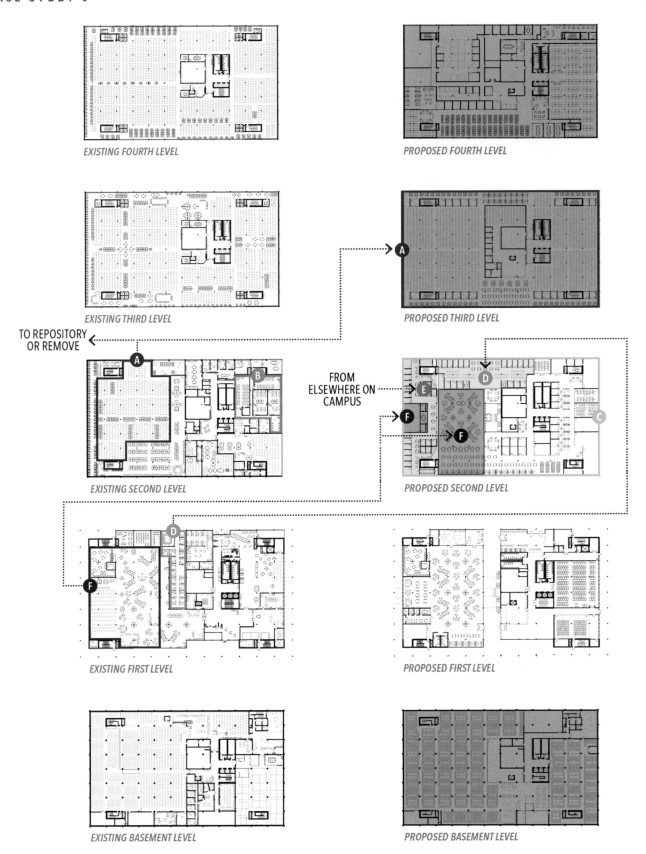

EXISTING FOURTH LEVEL

PROPOSED FOURTH LEVEL

EXISTING THIRD LEVEL

PROPOSED THIRD LEVEL

TO REPOSITORY OR REMOVE

FROM ELSEWHERE ON CAMPUS

EXISTING SECOND LEVEL

PROPOSED SECOND LEVEL

EXISTING FIRST LEVEL

PROPOSED FIRST LEVEL

EXISTING BASEMENT LEVEL

PROPOSED BASEMENT LEVEL

Figure 7.74. Case Study 6: Phasing plans

PHASE 5

A Create a temporary entrance through the east facade to allow public access to elevators, stairs, and toilets during the renovation of the main level.

B Close the café. Renovate the main level in its entirety, except for the temporary entrance and the recently renovated tutoring space.

C After the renovation of the main level, move tutoring, ITS, and computer commons functions (temporarily located on the second level in step F of phase 4) to their final locations on the main level.

D Once new main entry is opened, remove temporary entrance and complete the renovation of main level.

NOTE :
The gray shaded regions represent areas renovated in previous phases.

Figure 7.75. Case Study 6: Phasing plans

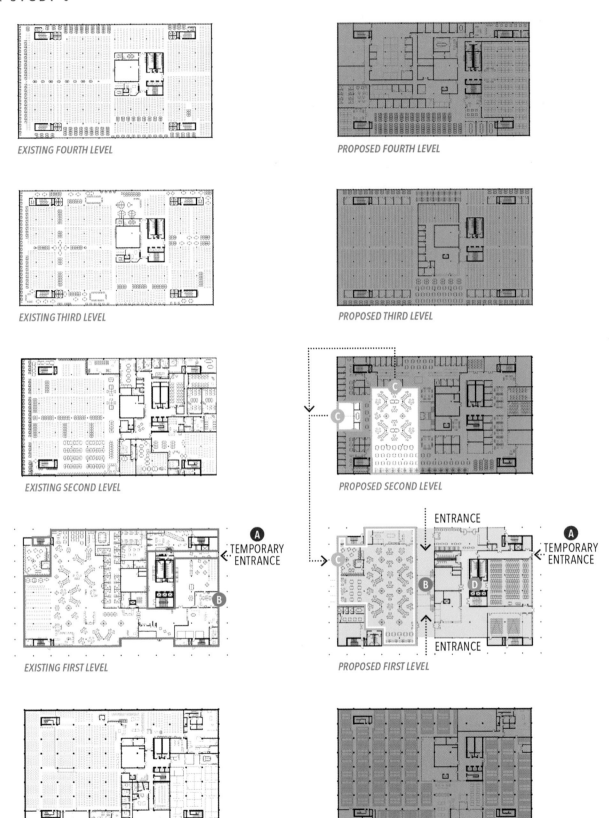

EXISTING FOURTH LEVEL

PROPOSED FOURTH LEVEL

EXISTING THIRD LEVEL

PROPOSED THIRD LEVEL

EXISTING SECOND LEVEL

PROPOSED SECOND LEVEL

EXISTING FIRST LEVEL

PROPOSED FIRST LEVEL

EXISTING BASEMENT LEVEL

PROPOSED BASEMENT LEVEL

Figure 7.76. Case Study 6: Phasing plans

BIBLIOGRAPHY

Barclay, Donald A., and Eric D. Scott. 2011. *The Library Renovation, Maintenance, and Construction Handbook.* New York: Neal-Schuman.

Charbonnet, Lisa. 2015. *Public Library Buildings: The Librarian's Go-To Guide for Construction, Expansion, and Renovation Projects.* Santa Barbara, CA: Libraries Unlimited.

Dewe, Michael. 2017. *Planning Public Library Buildings: Concepts and Issues for the Librarian.* New York: Taylor & Francis.

Huckaby, Hank. 2011. "Chancellor Huckaby's Report to the Board of Regents." Office of the Chancellor, University System of Georgia, September 14, accessed July 2017. https://web.archive.org/web/20111104063622/http://www.usg.edu:80/chancellor/speeches/chancellor_huckabys_report_to_the_board_of_regents.

Leighton, Philip A., and David C. Weber. 1999. *Planning Academic and Research Library Buildings.* 3rd edition. Chicago: ALA Editions.

Library Leadership & Management Association, eds. 2011. *Building Blocks for Planning Functional Library Space.* 3rd edition. Lanham, MD: Scarecrow Press.

Lushington, Nolan. 2002. *Libraries Designed for Users: A 21st Century Guide.* New York: Neal-Schuman.

McArthur, John A., and Valerie J. Graham. 2015. "User-Experience Design and Library Spaces: A Pathway to Innovation?" *Journal of Library Innovation* 6, no. 2: 1–14.

Miller, Rebecca T., and Barbara A. Genco, eds. 2016. *Better Library Design: Ideas from Library Journal.* Lanham, MD: Rowman & Littlefield.

Murphy, Tish. 2007. *Library Furnishings: A Planning Guide.* Jefferson, NC: McFarland.

Oldenburg, Ray. 1999. *The Great Good Place: Cafés, Coffee Shops, Bookstores, Bars, Hair Salons, and Other Hangouts at the Heart of a Community.* New York: Marlowe.

———. 2001. *Celebrating the Third Place: Inspiring Stories about the "Great Good Places" at the Heart of Our Communities.* New York: Marlowe.

Piotrowicz, Lisa M., and Scott Osgood. 2010. *Building Science 101: A Primer for Librarians.* Chicago: ALA Editions.

Robinson, Meyer. 2016. "Fewer Americans Are Visiting Local Libraries—and Technology Isn't to Blame." *Atlantic,* April 14. Accessed October 2017. www.theatlantic.com/technology/archive/2016/04/americans-like-their-libraries-but-they-use-them-less-and-less-pew/477336.

Sannwald, William W. 2015. *Checklist of Library Building Design Considerations.* 6th edition. Chicago: ALA Editions.

Stewart, Christopher. 2010. *The Academic Library Building in the Digital Age: A Study of Construction, Planning, and Design of New Library Space.* Chicago: Association of College and Research Libraries.

Wall, Kay. 2011. "Clemson's Road Map." *Library Journal* 136, no. 19: 30–34.

Watson, Les, ed. 2009. *Better Library and Learning Spaces: Projects, Trends and Ideas.* Chicago: ALA Editions.

INDEX

ABOUT THE AUTHORS

David R. Moore II, AIA, ALA, LEED AP BD+C, NCARB, is a principal and the Higher Education Studio leader at McMillan Pazdan Smith Architecture who also leads the firm's dedicated Library Design Team. He holds a Master of Architecture degree from Clemson University and resides in Greenville, South Carolina. For more than twenty-five years David has worked exclusively with libraries. He is an accomplished speaker and lecturer on library design and sustainability and is responsible for the design of many award-winning libraries throughout the Southeast. David has also authored numerous library building programs, feasibility studies, and Road Maps for academic, public, and private institutions across the country.

David's clients include Clemson University, Louisiana State University, University of Wisconsin—Milwaukee, UNC Asheville, Western Carolina University, San José State University/San José Public Library, Kennesaw State University, University of the South, the Westminster Schools in Atlanta, and numerous public library systems throughout the Southeast, including the Richland Library in Columbia, South Carolina.

David's work has been featured in national publications including *Contract* magazine, *American Libraries*, *College Planning & Management*, and *Library Journal*. He has been a featured speaker at regional and national SCUP, APPA, NACUBO, PLA, and ALA conferences throughout the country and has also spoken at dozens of state and regional library conferences including SELA, SCLA, and COMO.

Eric Shoaf, MLS, MPA, is dean of the library at Queens University of Charlotte. He has thirty years' experience working in five different library systems of varying sizes, and over the past fifteen years he has been heavily involved in library building and renovation projects at a variety of libraries. Eric has specialized experience in library public services, special collections, print and media storage, and administration of library budgets. He is widely published in the library literature and previously served as editor for *Library Leadership & Management*, the journal published by the American Library Association's LLAMA division. He has been a speaker about library renovation and partnership with architects and space planners at national conferences. Eric has a BA from Duke University and master's degrees from the University of Rhode Island and North Carolina Central University. He resides in Charlotte, North Carolina.